M A R G A R E T   M

101 Career Alternatives
for Teachers

*Exciting Job Opportunities
for Teachers Outside the
Teaching Profession*

P R I M A   P U B L I S H I N G

Published by Prima Publishing, Roseville, California. Member of the Crown Publishing Group, a division of Random House, Inc.

PRIMA PUBLISHING and colophon are trademarks of Random House, Inc., registered with the United States Patent and Trademark Office.

Every effort has been made to make this book complete and accurate as of the date of publication. In a time of rapid change, however, it is difficult to ensure that all information is entirely up-to-date. Although the publisher and author cannot be liable for any inaccuracies or omissions in this book, they are always grateful for corrections and suggestions for improvement.

Library of Congress Cataloging-in-Publication Data on File
ISBN 0-7615-3452-0

01 02 03 04 HH 10 9 8 7 6 5 4 3 2 1
Printed in the United States of America

First Edition

Visit us online at www.primapublishing.com

CONTENTS

CHAPTER TEN
Publish or Perish   261

CHAPTER ELEVEN
Let the Games Begin!   293

CHAPTER TWELVE
Developing the Plan   321

CHAPTER ONE

You're in Good Company

Teaching is one of the world's oldest professions. Throughout history, it has always provided a sense of fellowship and accomplishment for the many who chose to be educators. Ancient Roman professors were as popular in their time as Madonna and Tom Cruise are today. Yet that sentiment toward teachers and the teaching profession has now changed significantly.

Why Are Teachers Leaving the Profession?

One big problem facing our education system is the defection of many teachers to other careers. The Department of Education estimates that more than one million new teachers will be needed before the year 2010. That's nearly half the number of elementary and secondary school teachers working today.

In addition to the job's lack of prestige, a major reason for these mass defections is the wage gap between teaching and other professions. Workers who have master's degrees in other fields earn an average of $25,000 more per year than teachers who have master's degrees. In

1998, teachers aged 22 to 28 with bachelor's degrees earned an average of $23,000 per year, while those with the same degree in other fields earned $40,000 per year. Teachers aged 44 to 50 with master's degrees earned just over $40,000 per year, while their counterparts in other professions earned nearly $80,000 per year. This wage gap does not seem likely to decrease. Since 1995, teachers' pay scales have increased just 11 percent, the lowest of any professional field.

Poor earning potential, along with added stress caused by larger classrooms and increased responsibilities in and out of the classroom, have led to record numbers of teachers seeking work elsewhere. Fortunately, educators enjoy widespread opportunities to transfer teaching skills to alternate careers.

Making the leap from a familiar career into something new is not easy. Perhaps a radical change is not for you, but if you feel unappreciated and underpaid, maybe this is exactly what you need. This book contains 101 possible alternatives to your current profession. Some careers offer the prospect of travel and adventure, while others offer the opportunity to be your own boss. They all, however, are a departure from the rigors of teaching in elementary and secondary schools.

To assist you in finding a new career, each job entry contains the following information:

- Definition—Technical definition of the job
- Transferable Teaching Skills—Three skills that link the new job to teaching
- Necessary Skills—Description of skills needed to succeed in the field
- Success Tips—Pointers on how to succeed in this field
- 9 to 5: How You Will Spend Your Day—Basic description of the daily responsibilities of the job
- Where You Will Spend Your Day—Description of the expected work environment
- Career Forecast—Job outlook information and forecast
- Monetary Rewards—Earning potential and possible benefits

- Up the Ladder—Career advancement information
- Related Jobs—Similar jobs that require similar skills or interests
- Gathering More Facts—Additional sources of information about specific fields via addresses, telephone numbers, and Web sites
- From Classroom to . . . —As an added feature, some of the job descriptions include personal information from someone actually in the field.

The jobs mentioned in this book are just a few of the possibilities open to teachers taking their skills into new careers. We hope that the information will help you decide if a career switch is right for you.

Whether you embark on a new career or remain in the teaching profession, we wish you the best of luck.

Before You Decide

After four years of college, countless graduate courses, and following in the footsteps of Plato and Socrates, you now realize that teaching is not what you had envisioned. You feel that a better career choice might exist in another field. But now comes the difficult part: finding a new career that will motivate and challenge you into fulfilling your dream.

You should consider your answers to the following questions before embarking on a job quest. No matter how you respond, your answers will contain valuable clues to guide your career move.

1. Why do you want to leave teaching?
2. What factor or factors caused you to make this decision?
3. What do you seek that you haven't found in your current teaching career?
4. What satisfactions do you hope to gain from your career change?

5. How long have you seriously considered making a change?
6. Is a single issue or event pushing or encouraging you to leave, or has the situation been building up for a while?
7. Is the school corporation bringing on the change?
8. Are you tired of battling with parents?
9. Do you dislike being a constant disciplinarian?
10. Do you dislike taking work home?
11. Are you tired of taking college classes to keep your license current?
12. Are you looking for tangible or intangible benefits from the move?
13. Whom do you seek for advice or consultation?
14. Who will be affected by this career change?
15. What additional training, education, or both will you require if you make this career change?
16. Why not try?
17. What do you have to lose by exploring other opportunities?
18. What are the future opportunities in your new career?

Always keep in mind that the best time to search for a new career is when you are already employed. You are more marketable and desirable when you are employed.

You will have the opportunity to compare careers, and you won't be forced to take a new job unless you are very comfortable with it.

Evaluate Your Skills

Did you know that Bill Cosby has an education degree? He used his teaching skills to develop award-winning children's TV shows such as *Fat Albert* and *The Electric Company*. Although you may not want to develop educational television programs like Bill Cosby, you also possess skills from your teaching career that can be used in other fields. Many people don't realize that it takes time and effort to find a job they really enjoy. Knowing your skills will help you select a successful new career.

The following informal skills inventory can help you:

- Identify skills and abilities that can lead to a successful career
- Target more satisfying career paths
- Explore careers that you may not have thought about yet

Skills Inventory

Directions: After reading each statement, circle the number that corresponds with the description that best fits you: Never like me, not really like me, sometimes like me, usually like me, or always like me. Then follow the directions to score the inventory at the end of the form.

	NEVER LIKE ME	NOT REALLY LIKE ME	SOMETIMES LIKE ME	USUALLY LIKE ME	ALWAYS LIKE ME
1. I enjoy teaching others, including adults.	1	2	3	4	5
2. I like being in charge.	1	2	3	4	5
3. I enjoy working with numbers.	1	2	3	4	5
4. I have excellent speaking skills.	1	2	3	4	5
5. I can work in a team.	1	2	3	4	5
6. I am more of a leader than a follower.	1	2	3	4	5
7. I can handle stressful situations calmly.	1	2	3	4	5
8. I can think of unique ideas.	1	2	3	4	5
9. I like being outdoors.	1	2	3	4	5
10. I like to motivate and direct people to learn new things.	1	2	3	4	5
11. I can manage more than one project at a time.	1	2	3	4	5
12. I can analyze data into meaningful ideas.	1	2	3	4	5
13. I am comfortable speaking to an audience.	1	2	3	4	5
14. I like to use a computer to get a job done.	1	2	3	4	5

15. I am very ambitious.	1	2	3	4	5
16. I like looking for ways to help people.	1	2	3	4	5
17. I enjoy working independently.	1	2	3	4	5
18. I have the ability to coach others.	1	2	3	4	5
19. I enjoy helping others even if they make many mistakes.	1	2	3	4	5
20. I don't mind being an authoritarian.	1	2	3	4	5
21. I enjoy working in an office.	1	2	3	4	5
22. I have a good speaking voice.	1	2	3	4	5
23. I like solving complex problems.	1	2	3	4	5
24. I am a self-starter.	1	2	3	4	5
25. I can make good decisions based on known information.	1	2	3	4	5
26. I have an excellent grasp of the English language.	1	2	3	4	5
27. Adventurous outings are exciting to me.	1	2	3	4	5
28. I like working with a group.	1	2	3	4	5
29. I am able to negotiate to get tasks accomplished.	1	2	3	4	5
30. I have a good sense of finance.	1	2	3	4	5
31. I have excellent oral communication skills.	1	2	3	4	5
32. I have good keyboarding skills.	1	2	3	4	5
33. I have very good organizational skills.	1	2	3	4	5
34. I can handle emotional people.	1	2	3	4	5
35. I can handle the pressure of deadlines.	1	2	3	4	5

(continues)

	NEVER LIKE ME	NOT REALLY LIKE ME	SOMETIMES LIKE ME	USUALLY LIKE ME	ALWAYS LIKE ME
36. I enjoy being physically active.	1	2	3	4	5
37. I can assess others' abilities and place them in a group.	1	2	3	4	5
38. I can come up with different ways to solve a problem.	1	2	3	4	5
39. I can talk to others and effectively convey information.	1	2	3	4	5
40. I have good written communication skills.	1	2	3	4	5
41. I like to keep up-to-date on the latest technology.	1	2	3	4	5
42. I am a risk-taker.	1	2	3	4	5
43. I am diplomatic.	1	2	3	4	5
44. I can remain focused on a task for an extended time period.	1	2	3	4	5
45. I like to travel.	1	2	3	4	5
46. I am a good judge of how well someone is learning or doing.	1	2	3	4	5
47. I am assertive.	1	2	3	4	5
48. I can gather information and determine what is essential.	1	2	3	4	5
49. I enjoy talking.	1	2	3	4	5
50. I am persistent when faced with a problem.	1	2	3	4	5
51. I enjoy a challenge.	1	2	3	4	5
52. I can keep others' personal information confidential.	1	2	3	4	5
53. I can gather information by observing.	1	2	3	4	5
54. I am outgoing.	1	2	3	4	5
55. I am patient.	1	2	3	4	5

56. I can make a decision and be confident it is the right one.	1	2	3	4	5
57. I can listen to people and ask questions to determine needs.	1	2	3	4	5
58. I am fluent in a language other than English.	1	2	3	4	5
59. I can work with little supervision.	1	2	3	4	5
60. I like doing things my own way.	1	2	3	4	5
61. I am able to persuade others to approach things differently.	1	2	3	4	5
62. I am self-motivated.	1	2	3	4	5
63. I like helping others reach their fullest potential.	1	2	3	4	5
64. I enjoy using different approaches when teaching new things.	1	2	3	4	5
65. I can competently manage a budget.	1	2	3	4	5
66. I am able to use mathematics to solve problems.	1	2	3	4	5
67. I am able to manage my own time and the time of others.	1	2	3	4	5
68. I have a strong interest in computers and technology.	1	2	3	4	5
69. I don't mind working long hours.	1	2	3	4	5
70. I can empathize with others' personal struggles.	1	2	3	4	5
71. I pay much attention to detail.	1	2	3	4	5
72. I am energetic.	1	2	3	4	5

Scoring the Skills Inventory

UNUSUAL TEACHING SITUATIONS

Add together the numbers circled for questions:

____ 1	____ 37
____ 10	____ 46
____ 19	____ 55
____ 28	____ 64 **Total** _____

If your total is 35–40, then read about the career ideas in chapter 1, "Unusual Teaching Situations."

BEING IN CHARGE

Add together the numbers circled for questions:

____ 2	____ 38
____ 11	____ 47
____ 20	____ 56
____ 29	____ 65 **Total** _____

If your total is 35–40, then read about the career ideas in chapter 2, "Being in Charge."

THE BUSINESS WORLD

Add together the numbers circled for questions:

____ 3	____ 39
____ 12	____ 48
____ 21	____ 57
____ 30	____ 66 **Total** _____

If your total is 35–40, then read about the career ideas in chapter 3, "The Business World."

USING COMMUNICATION SKILLS

Add together the numbers circled for questions:

____ 4	____ 40	
____ 13	____ 49	
____ 22	____ 58	
____ 31	____ 67	Total _____

If your total is 35–40, then read about the career ideas in chapter 4, "Using Communication Skills."

COMPUTERS 'R' US

Add together the numbers circled for questions:

____ 5	____ 41	
____ 14	____ 50	
____ 23	____ 59	
____ 32	____ 68	Total _____

If your total is 35–40, then read about the career ideas in chapter 5, "Computers 'R' Us."

THE ENTREPRENEUR'S LIFE

Add together the numbers circled for questions:

____ 6	____ 42	
____ 15	____ 51	
____ 24	____ 60	
____ 33	____ 69	Total _____

If your total is 35–40, then read about the career ideas in chapter 6, "The Entrepreneur's Life."

THE NOBLE PUBLIC SERVANT

Add together the numbers circled for questions:

____ 7	____ 43
____ 16	____ 52
____ 25	____ 61
____ 34	____ 70 Total _____

If your total is 35–40, then read about the career ideas in chapter 8, "The Noble Public Servant."

PUBLISH OR PERISH

Add together the numbers circled for questions:

____ 8	____ 44
____ 17	____ 53
____ 26	____ 62
____ 35	____ 71 Total _____

If your total is 35–40, then read about the career ideas in chapter 9, "Publish or Perish."

LET THE GAMES BEGIN!

Add together the numbers circled for questions:

____ 9	____ 45
____ 18	____ 54
____ 27	____ 63
____ 36	____ 72 Total _____

If your total is 35–40, then read about the career ideas in chapter 10, "Let the Games Begin!"

If your total score is **less than 18** for each of the previous sections, then read about the career ideas in chapter 7, "And Now for Something Completely Different."

Consider This

If you think of going into sales, keep in mind that most sales openings do not require a certain degree or years of experience. They almost all require good communication skills and being able to work well with all types of people. In sales, people are hired for their personality rather than for their academic degree or experience. You already possess some of the essential skills to undertake a sales job.

Unusual Teaching Situations

Because you have selected this book to read, chances are you're a teacher. Before looking at other careers, though, did you realize just how many different opportunities exist within the teaching field? You may be unhappy with your location, the subject that you teach, or the age of your students. You can make a few changes, be on a different career path, and still remain in the teaching profession.

Are you looking for adventure? Have you thought about teaching overseas or in a prison facility? Maybe you'd like to stay in the same school corporation. Have you considered a different grade level or a whole different subject area? Maybe you teach music now, but if you took a few classes you could teach first grade or high school orchestra. The jobs described in this chapter will allow you to remain in the teaching profession. You will still be in front of a group of students and still be able to influence their lives with the material you present. As you consider your options, the information in this chapter will help you make an important career decision.

1. *School Counselor*

DEFINITION

School counselors assist students with situations that concern academic and personal development.

TRANSFERABLE TEACHING SKILLS

- Active listening
- Strong interpersonal skills
- Questioning

NECESSARY SKILLS

- Trustworthiness
- Communication skills
- Attentiveness

SUCCESS TIPS

- Verbalize your ideas effectively
- Clearly hear what someone is saying
- Help people resolve problems

9 TO 5: HOW YOU WILL SPEND YOUR DAY

School counselors are just as responsible for the academic and personal success of students as teachers are. They assist students in the selection of classes and may offer advice about extracurricular activities. They work with students in selecting career goals and pursuing the courses needed to achieve these goals. To establish goals, counselors might need to assess students' skills, interests, and personal traits.

Counselors help students deal with family or personal problems, which can warrant counselors meeting with students' parents. They also may be required to provide drug or alcohol program information. Counselors are part of a collec-

From Classroom to . . .

Gary Sailors, a former middle school teacher and now a *high school counselor,* believes it is important for counselors to take advantage of professional development opportunities.

"I'm a more effective counselor because I try to keep up-to-date on what's going on in the counseling field. Improving my skills means I can better help my students."

Gary recognizes that a counselor must be an excellent communicator and have strong listening skills.

"I often find myself in situations with students, parents, or even colleagues, in which I must listen carefully to help resolve a problem. I need to hear the facts, as well as the feelings involved, so I can help individuals make decisions they are comfortable with."

tive effort to help the student, which includes teachers, school psychologists, school nurses, and parents.

Students wishing to get into college may also use the assistance of school counselors. The counselors can become liaisons between students and actual college recruiters. They help students obtain information about scholarships, undergraduate universities or colleges, and vocational and technical schools.

WHERE YOU WILL SPEND YOUR DAY

School counselors work long, irregular hours, due mainly to the constant need to meet with students before and after school hours. Counselors have their own offices, which are usually on school grounds. For the most part, counselors spend all of their work hours on site at school.

CAREER FORECAST

Employment for school counselors is expected to grow in response to higher enrollment. Schools will need more personnel to help students deal with a multitude of difficult issues, like drug and alcohol abuse, death, and suicide. However, budget cuts could slow the growth of opportunities for school counselors.

MONETARY REWARDS

Earnings for a school counselor average about $25,000 per year, but that depends greatly on the counselor's geographical location and experience. Experienced counselors earn between $38,500 and $45,000 a year. Benefits include health insurance, paid holidays and vacations, sick leave, and retirement plans. Counselors may also use the summer months as a paid vacation.

UP THE LADDER

School counselors may specialize in certain areas of guidance and may concentrate on just those. This could lead to their being designated resident experts in particular areas. Advancement could come in the form of gaining an administrator's position in the school system.

RELATED JOBS

- College student personnel worker
- Occupational therapist
- Social worker

GATHERING MORE FACTS

American Counseling Association
5999 Stevenson Avenue
Alexandria, Virginia 22304-3300
Phone: (800) 347-6647
Internet: www.counseling.org

American School Counselor Association
801 North Fairfax Street, Suite 310
Alexandria, VA 22314

Phone: (703) 683-2722
Internet: www.schoolcounselor.org

National Board for Certified Counselors, Inc.
3 Terrace Way, Suite D
Greensboro, NC 27403-3660 USA
Internet: www.nbcc.org

2. *College Professor*

DEFINITION

College professors teach undergraduate and graduate students in colleges and universities.

TRANSFERABLE TEACHING SKILLS

- Supervising
- Verbalizing
- Instructing

NECESSARY SKILLS

- Communication
- Integrating
- Developing

SUCCESS TIPS

- Be able to give interesting lectures
- Have good organizational skills
- Cultivate time-management skills

9 TO 5: HOW YOU WILL SPEND YOUR DAY

College professors teach in two-year community colleges, four-year universities, or colleges and graduate and professional schools. Most professors work in one specific department, and some specialize in one area of their discipline. Generally, college professors teach between two and four classes each semester. They use various styles of teaching, but most use the lecture format as their main method. In addition to teaching, professors maintain office hours for student accessibility.

Although all professors are considered professionals, there are three ranks in the profession. Instructors are the lowest level of college professors. Generally, they have very little job security and are not involved in deciding school curriculum or university policies. Instructors generally teach the undergraduate students. Assistant professors or associate professors have more experience than instructors. They generally teach undergraduate students but may teach graduate students at some schools. They are typically allowed active involvement in administrative decisions and are able to establish their own curriculums. Full professors are the most experienced of the three ranks. They sometimes serve as heads of departments, in addition to their regular teaching duties.

Many colleges and universities take advantage of high technology tools as a way to instruct, as well as to present, materials. Therefore, college professors must be comfortable learning about and using technology in their classrooms.

WHERE YOU WILL SPEND YOUR DAY

College professors usually teach in a room on a college campus, but with today's higher education reaching out into communities, many college teachers may find themselves teaching in a shopping center mall or an empty studio to students listening on different satellite stations.

This is a great job if you enjoy having a flexible schedule and not working 9 to 5. Because classes need to be taught in the evening and on weekends, many college professors actually have most of their days free. However, they have other obligations, such as holding office hours and attending meetings with the department chairs.

CAREER FORECAST

Career opportunities for college professors will grow rapidly over the next several years. This is due partly to the burgeoning 18- to 24-year-old population. Despite this increased need for college instructors, colleges and universities are looking to hire part-time teachers as a way to control costs.

Opportunities will be best for instructors with a background or experience in computer science, business, or engineering.

MONETARY REWARDS

College and university teachers earn approximately $46,600 per year. Teachers in public institutions earn an average of $56,000 per year, while those in private institutions make about $64,000 per year. Earnings for full-time instructors in four-year institutions are higher than for those teaching in two-year institutions.

Many university and college instructors have additional earnings from writing books or articles for professional periodicals. They may teach additional courses, complete research, or have some other type of employment.

UP THE LADDER

Some colleges and universities may offer professors the opportunity to be tenured. Tenured professors cannot be fired without just cause and due process. This allows professors to freely teach and conduct research and provides stability and security in employment. Many colleges and universities opt to hire part-time and limited-term contract faculty as a way to control expenses. Professors may pursue career opportunities as department chairpersons or deans as a means of advancement.

RELATED JOBS

- Librarian
- Writer
- Lobbyist

GATHERING MORE FACTS

American Association of University Professors
1012 Fourteenth Street, NW, Suite 500
Washington, DC 20005-3465
Phone: (202) 737-5900
Internet: www.aaup.org

American Federation of Teachers
555 New Jersey Avenue, NW
Washington, DC 20001
Phone: (202) 879-4400
Internet: www.aft.org

U.S. Department of Education
Office of Postsecondary Education
1990 K Street, NW
Washington, DC 20006
Internet: www.ed.gov/offices/OPE

3. *Prison Facility Teacher*

DEFINITION

Prison facility teachers instruct prisoners who are seeking a
high school diploma, GED, or college degree.

TRANSFERABLE TEACHING SKILLS

- Active listening
- Strong interpersonal skills
- Monitoring

NECESSARY SKILLS

- Instructing
- Good communication
- Patience and understanding

SUCCESS TIPS

- Use multiple approaches to teaching
- Develop an environment for safe learning
- Handle stressful situations in a calm manner

9 TO 5: HOW YOU WILL SPEND YOUR DAY

A prison facility teacher's day begins with a security check upon arrival. The teachers will likely have their belongings searched for contraband, will pass through a metal detector, and may even be subject to a pat-down search before entering the facility.

When teachers get to their classrooms, they may have to unlock cabinets, drawers, or desks that were secured at the end of the previous day. There may be staff meetings to attend, reports to submit, or student papers to grade. Teachers may have lesson plans to work on. Some teachers have multiple plans because they instruct learners at various levels.

Some teachers will teach in Pre-GED or Adult Basic Education classrooms, in which learners work up to the eighth-grade level. Others teach in a General Educational Development (GED) classroom, where students work from the eighth-grade to the twelfth-grade levels. In both types of classrooms, students learn at different levels, requiring the teacher to prepare materials appropriate for each person's ability.

Some people in a prison classroom will be very motivated to learn; others may be required to be present. It is important for the teacher to be patient, tolerant, and creative, to encourage and motivate each learner. At the end of the day, the teacher may have to secure cabinets, drawers, and desks to prevent theft. The teacher may even have to complete an inventory of the room to ensure that inmates took nothing during the day.

Prison facility teachers may be required to complete extensive training at the prison. This training will be similar to that received by the correctional officers, which instructs on security procedures, how to interact with inmates, and even how to restrain unruly inmates.

WHERE YOU WILL SPEND YOUR DAY

Prison facility teachers usually teach in a classroom located within the facility. It may be similar to classrooms in a regular school, with chalkboards, desks, or tables. Some older prisons may have limited classroom space, creating a less-than-optimal learning environment.

CAREER FORECAST

The need for prison facility teachers will likely increase in the near future, as more prisons are built to help relieve overcrowding. Budget constraints may slow the need for teachers somewhat, because the money will be redirected to hiring more security staff.

MONETARY REWARDS

Prison facility teachers typically earn higher wages than public school teachers because of the potentially dangerous environment. Annual earnings range between $35,500 and $39,800.

UP THE LADDER

Advancement comes in the form of teachers taking on additional responsibilities. Some choose to pursue supervisory or administrative positions within the prison's education department.

RELATED JOBS

- Adult and vocational education teacher
- Social worker
- Probation officer

GATHERING MORE FACTS

Correctional Education Association
4380 Forbes Boulevard

Lanham, MD 20706
Phone: (301) 918-1915
Internet: www.ceanational.org

National Education Association
1201 16th Street, NW
Washington, DC 20030

U.S. Department of Education
Office of Correctional Education
400 Maryland Avenue, SW
MES 4527
Washington, DC 20202-7242
Internet: www.ed.gov/offices/OVAE/OCE

4. Adult and Vocational Education Teacher

DEFINITION

Adult education teachers instruct adults who have returned to school in order to learn basic skills or occupational skills.

TRANSFERABLE TEACHING SKILLS

- Instructing
- Listening
- Monitoring

NECESSARY SKILLS

- Work experience or knowledge of skill area to be taught
- Strong communication skills
- Patience and understanding

SUCCESS TIPS

- Use multiple approaches to teaching
- Develop an environment for safe learning
- Further your teaching skills through professional development seminars or conferences

9 TO 5: HOW YOU WILL SPEND YOUR DAY

An adult education teacher may teach basic skills to adult learners. These include reading, writing, and math. Learners may be in a Pre-GED or an Adult Basic Education class, which typically works with learners through the eighth-grade level. Adults learning through the twelfth-grade level are preparing for the General Educational Development (GED) test. The GED is the equivalent to a high school diploma.

Adult vocational-technical teachers teach occupational skills, such as welding, auto mechanics, or x-ray technician skills. Some teach skills that help the learners keep up with technological advances in order to maintain their jobs or seek better jobs.

Adult and vocational education teachers work with adults who attend classes by choice. These individuals want to learn. This makes the teaching experience much different from teaching in a public school setting. These adults are highly motivated. The challenge comes in working with students of different levels at the same time. A teacher may have someone who is just beginning to read and another working at an eighth-grade level in the same classroom. An adult education teacher has to be flexible and able to change gears quickly to work with a wide variety of learners. Some learners may need extra attention because they lack good study skills or self-confidence. Patience and understanding are important qualities in an adult education teacher.

WHERE YOU WILL SPEND YOUR DAY

Most adult and vocational education teachers teach in a classroom. Others teach on site at companies that offer adult education courses to their employees. Classrooms may be large, well lit, and fully equipped with comfortable tables, desks, and chairs; may have an abundance of learning materials and resources; or may have modern computer systems for students' use. At the other end of the spectrum, adult literacy organizations with limited budgets may have to share classroom space with other organizations. The classroom could be set up wherever space is available. The instructor may even need to bring in learning materials.

Many adult and vocational teachers work only part time. They often must conduct classes at night and on weekends to accommodate the learners' schedules.

CAREER FORECAST

Job opportunities as an adult and vocational education teacher will continue to grow. The best positions will go to individuals with certification in computer technology, auto mechanics, and other high-paying fields.

MONETARY REWARDS

The average yearly salary for adult education teachers is $25,000. Vocational education teachers earn about $34,500. Earnings vary by region of the country and the subject area taught. Teachers with better credentials receive higher earnings. Part-time teachers are usually paid an hourly rate and do not receive benefits.

UP THE LADDER

Some adult and vocational education teachers will advance to administrative positions within the organization. Teachers who work for businesses may advance to company training departments. Some teachers even go out on their own as consultants and contract with businesses to offer adult education classes on site.

From Classroom to . . .

It was a big adjustment for Felicitas Hubbard when she decided to leave her special education classroom at a state school for the blind, to take a job as an *institutional teacher* at a level three correctional facility. "I soon found out that teachers are greatly needed at prisons because many inmates cannot read or write."

The job can be stressful because of many problems prison students face, such as alcohol or drug addiction and mental health issues, along with overcrowding and understaffing. "Along with that is the pressure that I always need to be aware that some of my students have a dangerous background and that there is a risk of being injured on the job by one of these men."

Even so, Felicitas feels a great sense of satisfaction, knowing that she has a demanding job that will benefit society. "That's what makes this a rewarding experience."

RELATED JOBS

- Counselor
- Public relations specialist
- Social worker

GATHERING MORE FACTS

Association for Career and Technical Education
1410 King Street
Alexandria, VA 22314
Internet: www.acteonline.org

U.S. Department of Education
Office of Vocational and Adult Education
4090 MES
400 Maryland Avenue, SW

Washington, DC 20202
Phone: (202) 205-5451
Fax: (202) 205-8748
Internet: www.ed.gov/offices/OVAE

National Dissemination Center for Career and
    Technical Education
1900 Kenny Road
Columbus, OH 43210-1090
Phone: (800) 678-6011
Internet: www.nccte.com

5. *School Media Specialist*

DEFINITION

School media specialists instruct and advise educational institutions on the use of nonprint media.

TRANSFERABLE TEACHING SKILLS

- Instructing
- Inspiring
- Verbalizing

NECESSARY SKILLS

- Organizing
- Communication skills
- Ability to integrate

SUCCESS TIPS

- Create effective programs
- Implement your ideas
- Organize people to work together

9 TO 5: HOW YOU WILL SPEND YOUR DAY

Either a school district or an individual school may employ a school media specialist. Specialists who work for school districts have administrative responsibilities. They decide on the use of all audiovisual materials for the schools in their district. Specialists also create policies on the use of nonprint materials in the schools.

Specialists who work for individual schools assist teachers in planning individual programs for their classes. For example, a media specialist may consult with a physical education teacher about posters, books, and films about sports and health for a gym class. Media specialists are also involved with planning the school's curriculum.

They present training sessions about the use of nonprint media in classrooms for teachers and school officials. They are aware of all the equipment available for use and supervise the buying of additional equipment.

WHERE YOU WILL SPEND YOUR DAY

Many specialists work in school libraries and work regular school hours. Media specialists in public libraries and college and university libraries might work weekends, evenings, and some holidays. Overtime is sometimes necessary.

CAREER FORECAST

The increasing use of technology and library automation equipment is expected to cause a growth in the need for school media specialists. Budget constraints could slow the growth somewhat.

MONETARY REWARDS

School media specialists earn an average of $24,000 per year. Earnings depend on the wealth of the school system and the geographical location. Benefits usually include vacations, insurance, and pension plans.

UP THE LADDER

Media specialists advance by taking on additional responsibilities and by gaining experience. They may advance to supervisory positions within the school system.

RELATED JOBS

- Records clerk
- Medical record technician
- Title searcher

GATHERING MORE FACTS

American Library Association
Office for Human Resource Development and Recruitment
50 East Huron Street
Chicago, IL 60611
Internet: www.ala.org

Council on Library/Media Technicians
P.O. Box 951
Oxon Hill, MD 20750

Office of Educational Research and Improvement
    Library Program
Library Development Staff
U.S. Department of Education
555 New Jersey Avenue, NW, Room 402
Washington, DC 20208-5571

6. *Special Education Teacher*

DEFINITION

Special education teachers instruct students with various disabilities.

TRANSFERABLE TEACHING SKILLS

- Compassion
- Patience
- Structuring

NECESSARY SKILLS

- Communication
- Assessing
- Motivating

SUCCESS TIPS

- Be able to write an Individual Educational Program (IEP)
- Handle daily stress
- Keep current on all the federal and state laws that apply to special education

9 TO 5: HOW YOU WILL SPEND YOUR DAY

Special education teachers teach students with various disabilities, ranging from physical to learning or behavioral disabilities. They design learning plans structured to address each student's special needs. Special education teachers, along with social workers, school psychologists, and occupational, speech-language, and physical therapists, as well as parents, come together to develop an individual education plan (IEP) for each student. IEPs establish personal educational goals for all students, depending on their learning styles. Special education teachers tailor their students' instruction based on the students' disabilities. For example, if a student is blind, the teacher will use more audio-based learning tools.

Helping the student develop emotionally and socially is also the responsibility of special education teachers. Part of their job is to prepare students to function socially outside of their academic environment. Special education teachers regularly hold meetings with other educational professionals and the students' parents in an effort to encourage in-home learning and to inform parents of their children's academic performance.

In addition to working with students, special education teachers are responsible for various clerical tasks, such as completing governmental forms and preparing and grading student paperwork.

Where You Will Spend Your Day

Usually, your day will be spent in a classroom in a school building. However, openings exist for special education teachers at other sites, such as residential placement and inside prisons. Wherever your classroom is located, you will spend most of your day working with your students and helping them learn what they need to be productive in society. You will probably have a smaller number of students than in a normal classroom because of the many challenges you face daily.

Career Forecast

The job outlook is great because the demand for special education teachers will increase for the next several years. Currently, the need outweighs the number of special education teachers. Many teachers get into special education on provisional licenses. The requirements for a provisional license vary for each state. This is an opportunity for you to enter a different area of teaching, while only having to conduct a few classes per year.

Monetay Rewards

Special education teachers earn between $26,000 and $78,000 per year, depending on additional degrees and years of experience. Nearly 60 percent of special education teachers belong to the American Federation of Teachers and the National Education Association.

Up the Ladder

Special education teachers climb in their profession by earning advanced degrees so that they can obtain supervisory positions.

Related Jobs

- Social worker
- Rehabilitation counselor
- Physical education teacher

Gathering More Facts

Council for Exceptional Children
1110 North Glebe Road, Suite 300
Arlington, VA 22201-5704
Phone: (888) 232-7733
Internet: www.cec.sped.org

From Classroom to ...

Currently, many job openings exist in the *special education field*. Tricia Olsen is very glad that she returned to school to get an endorsement in Emotional Disabilities. She traded her classroom of twenty-three first-graders for a self-contained classroom of five very needy students with emotional disabilities. Two full-time assistants help her keep the children compliant with school policies.

"There are a lot of opportunities for teachers who go back to school to get licensed in any special education field. However, don't expect that you will have more energy at the end of the day because of a lower teacher/student ratio. Special education students require a great amount of patience, and their academic progress is often slow. That can be very frustrating. My job is very rewarding but definitely not easy."

Office of Special Education Programs
U.S. Department of Education
400 Maryland Avenue, SW
Washington, DC 20202
Phone: (202) 205-5507
Internet: www.ed.gov/offices/OSERS/OSEP

National Education Association
1201 16th Street, NW
Washington, DC 20036

7. *Teaching Overseas*

DEFINITION

Overseas teachers go to other countries around the world to teach.

TRANSFERABLE TEACHING SKILLS

- Instructing
- Monitoring
- Implementation planning

NECESSARY SKILLS

- Speaking skills
- Using creative learning strategies
- Critical thinking

SUCCESS TIPS

- Be open-minded and have a commitment to overseas education
- Be willing to take on the challenge of the unknown
- Be creative when materials are limited

9 TO 5: HOW YOU WILL SPEND YOUR DAY

About 250,000 school-age American children attend school overseas. Many are children of men and women serving in the armed forces who are stationed all over the world. The U.S. Department of Defense established and operates many of these schools. Children of civilian government officials and American-based businesses may also attend these schools. Many schools have been established by U.S. companies, church organizations, and private enterprises, which offer schooling for U.S. children. Some of these schools are open to the enrollment of nationals of all countries.

Overseas teaching jobs offer small classes (usually less than twenty-five students), excellent benefits, the opportunity to meet interesting people, and the chance to live in other countries around the world. Many schools offer outstanding staff development opportunities by enabling teachers to attend international conferences in various world capitals.

Most overseas schools focus on academics, with little opportunity for vocational or commercial education. The language used during instruction is English, but it is often supplemented with local language instruction. Teachers of these American-sponsored schools take advantage of their location and provide foreign language and local culture programs.

Teachers report that discipline problems rarely occur because the students come from families who have high expectations for their children in education. When a problem does arise, teachers almost always get complete support from the parents in resolving the problem. Children who are abroad obtain an unprecedented understanding of the world around them, as a result of living in another country.

WHERE YOU WILL SPEND YOUR DAY

American-sponsored schools range from tiny schools of less than 20 students to large schools with more than 2,600 students. Classrooms may be located in a rented house or on a campus. More and more organizations are occupying buildings constructed specifically for use as a school. Teachers usually have adequate instructional materials, although some countries' import laws or policies may delay needed supplies from the United States. The classroom teacher then has to be creative in instructional techniques. More American-sponsored schools are investing in quality computers and software to enhance learning.

CAREER FORECAST

Job opportunities for overseas teachers will continue to grow, as more U.S.-based companies expand operations overseas and U.S. government employees take their families to overseas job assignments. Also, more opportunities will exist because of the 10 to 25 percent turnover rate among overseas teachers and administrators.

MONETARY REWARDS

Salaries vary greatly—from $20,000 to $85,000 per year. Salaries in the Far East are often the highest, approaching $100,000 per year. Many positions are tax-free and most provide housing, travel, health insurance, and home leave. Overseas teachers with children can receive tuition-free enrollment. Schools typically offer a one- or two-year contract with an option to renew. Renewal bonuses of $1,000 to $2,000 are common.

UP THE LADDER

Many overseas schools offer numerous professional development opportunities, including conferences, workshops, and continuing education. Schools looking to fill administrative positions often hire from within, giving classroom teachers an excellent chance to advance their careers.

RELATED JOBS

- Special education teacher
- Social worker
- Public relations specialist

From Classroom to . . .

"I have met many wonderful people from all around the world," says Alison Kelsey. She began her *overseas teaching career* in 1996, after teaching English for eleven years in the United States.

"My husband, children, and I found the most difficult part of my first overseas assignment to be the separation from our families and friends. E-mail became our primary form of communication.

"I've had to be creative when dealing with the unexpected, such as teaching without electricity for several hours at a time or not having materials or supplies because of shipping delays.

"My family has had a lot of culture shock, but the whole experience has been well worth it."

GATHERING MORE FACTS

Association of International Educators
1307 New York Avenue, NW, 8th Floor
Washington, DC 20005-4701
Phone: (202) 737-3699
Internet: www.nafsa.org

The International Educator
P.O. Box 513
Cummaquid, MA 02637
Phone: (508) 365-1414
Internet: www.tieonline.com

United States Department of State
    Teaching Overseas Web site
Internet: www.state.gov/www/about state/schools
    /oteaching

Being in Charge

Whatever area or arena you teach in, you know how to be in charge. Your students respond to your directions. You are the leader of the group. At the same time, you're responsible to those higher on the educational ladder, such as the principal and superintendent.

This chapter's jobs are for people ready to move up the ladder or make a career switch out of education and into something with more management responsibilities. Returning to school for an administration license would give you the opportunity to run an entire school. You would take on a new role if you became the school principal. On the other hand, you might prefer to manage a store or an apartment complex. If you like being in charge, you will find many interesting career choices in this chapter.

8. *Adult Day-Care Coordinators*

DEFINITION

An adult day-care coordinator plans and implements special activities and routine daily living activities for adults.

Transferable Teaching Skills

- Organization
- Leadership
- Communication

Necessary Skills

- Compassion for the elderly and disabled
- Patience and the desire to help others
- Supervisory experience (at least one year) in a health or social setting

Success Tips

- Be able to coordinate activities that will interest adults
- Know how to supervise disparate groups of people
- Enjoy working with people

9 to 5: How You Will Spend Your Day

As an adult day-care coordinator, you'll ensure that the clients are well taken care of, which includes their hygiene concerns, medications, therapies, and social activities. Coordinators hire, train, and schedule the staff members who actually provide the caregiving. The coordinator also usually oversees food purchasing, meal planning, and food preparation, particularly for clients who have special dietary needs.

Adult day-care coordinators are particularly responsible for scheduling recreational activities and visitors for the clients. Activities range from crafts to games to parties for special occasions, such as holidays, birthdays, and volunteers.

Coordinators are also responsible for maintaining communication with the clients' families. Not only does the coordinator gather necessary care information from the family, but the coordinator also serves as an adviser to the family on the client's daily activities. Coordinators sometimes are required to take on other duties, such as fundraising or balancing the budget.

WHERE YOU WILL SPEND YOUR DAY

Most adult day-care coordinators work in one location for forty hours per week, Mondays through Fridays. They spend most of the day dealing with people throughout the center, either clients or staff.

CAREER FORECAST

Adult day care is one of the fastest-growing careers in human services—and will be until at least 2006—chiefly because of the swelling senior citizen population.

MONETARY REWARDS

Salary depends upon personal education, experience, and the day-care center's size and location, but it can range from $18,000 to $45,000, with full benefits.

UP THE LADDER

Advancement typically involves center growth, transfer to a larger center, starting a center, or pursuing other social work.

RELATED JOBS

- Adult instructor
- Social worker
- Recreation director

GATHERING MORE FACTS

American Geriatrics Society
770 Lexington Avenue, Suite 300
New York, NY 10021
Phone: (212) 308-1414
E-mail: info.arnger@americangeriatrics.org
Internet: www.americangeriatrics.org

National Association of Area Agencies on Aging
927 15th Street, NW, Sixth Floor
Washington, DC 20005
Phone: (202) 296-8130
Internet: www.n4a.org

National Institute on Aging
Building 31 Room 5C27
MSC 2292
Bethesda, MD 20892
Phone: (301) 496-1752
Internet: www.nih.gov/nia

9. *Property/Facilities Manager*

DEFINITION

Property managers supervise commercial and residential rental properties on a daily basis.

TRANSFERABLE TEACHING SKILLS

• Supervising
• Inspecting
• Maintaining

NECESSARY SKILLS

• Excellent communication skills
• Resourcefulness and creativity
• Excellent interpersonal skills, particularly in negotiations

SUCCESS TIPS

• Be able to work with people
• Implement rules fairly
• Observe potential problems before they occur

9 TO 5: HOW YOU WILL SPEND YOUR DAY

In some regions, a variety of people may own or rent small lots of property, office space, or living space. These people cannot be collectively responsible for the care and maintenance of the land beyond what they each currently use, so managers ensure that the property is maintained. Often, these managers supervise the maintenance of several properties at once, acting as agents and advisers for owners.

Property managers supervise the marketing of the property or portions of it, supervise bookkeeping, negotiate leases, and report property status to owners. Managers must negotiate maintenance, trash removal, snow removal, and other related services. Managers also hire on-site management for each property.

On-site managers oversee larger properties; they report directly to a property manager who oversees their work. On-site managers handle daily problems, keep records of operating costs, and organize maintenance staff. These managers deal directly with the residents or storeowners on a daily basis.

WHERE YOU WILL SPEND YOUR DAY

Property managers usually work in pleasant offices, but must regularly inspect the properties they manage. On-site managers also have pleasant offices, but must visit the various properties to ensure that all is running smoothly. Property managers often attend evening meetings with owners, boards of directors, and potential clients.

CAREER FORECAST

This career field is expected to grow about as fast as the average for all occupations. Individuals with college degrees will have the best opportunities.

MONETARY REWARDS

Salaries range from $12,000 to $60,700 a year, with an average of $28,500 a year. Property managers usually receive health insurance benefits, rent-free apartments, company automobiles, and possibly even part ownership in property development.

UP THE LADDER

Advancement comes with the responsibility of managing larger properties or perhaps through specializing in certain types of property. Some property managers may even be successful enough to establish their own companies.

RELATED JOBS

- Education administrator
- Health services manager
- Hotel and resort manager

GATHERING MORE FACTS

Building Owners and Managers Association International
1201 New York Avenue, NW, Suite 300
Washington, DC 20005
Phone: (202) 408-2662
Internet: www.boma.org

Community Associations Institute
1630 Duke Street
Alexandria, VA 22314
Phone: (703) 548-8600
Internet: www.caionline.org

Institute of Real Estate Management
430 North Michigan Avenue
Chicago, IL 60611
Phone: (312) 329-6000
Internet: www.irem.org

10. Child-Care Director

DEFINITION

A child-care director is responsible for all facets of the operation of a child-care center.

TRANSFERABLE TEACHING SKILLS

- Communication with parents
- Organization
- Social perceptiveness

NECESSARY SKILLS

- Leadership
- Budgeting
- Decisiveness

SUCCESS TIPS

- Be patient
- Stay physically fit
- Be flexible

9 TO 5: HOW YOU WILL SPEND YOUR DAY

Child-care directors have a wide range of duties. Their main responsibility is to ensure that the children receive the highest quality of care possible and that the teachers under their supervision are responsible and loving caregivers.

Child-care directors handle the enrollment of new children, order materials and supplies, conduct staff meetings, and attend parent-teacher conferences, as well as hire and fire teachers or other staff. Directors may have to fill in as substitute teachers or drive the day-care's van on field trips.

Because directors are ultimately responsible for the profit or loss of the day-care center, they often must actively market the center and make sure that tuition is paid for all children. The director may have to justify the operation of the center to a board of directors, owner, or group of owners.

Child-care directors who work for a day-care chain are responsible for carrying out the company's policies and daily procedures. They must be sure that all state regulations are followed. Finally, directors must ensure that the building is clean and properly maintained.

WHERE YOU WILL SPEND YOUR DAY

Child-care directors work in offices that are usually located in the day-care center. They might work in a classroom when a substitute teacher is needed. Directors usually work forty to fifty hours per week, Monday through Friday. Days and hours can vary, as more child-care centers offer night and weekend care.

CAREER FORECAST

Demand for good-quality child-care centers is high and will remain high. Federal and state governments are working to improve wages for child-care workers. In addition, welfare reform legislation and increased subsidization may cause some mothers to enter the workforce as their welfare benefits are decreased or eliminated.

MONETARY REWARDS

Child-care directors for day-care centers earn an average annual salary of $38,750. Benefits typically include vacations, insurance, and pension plans. Some for-profit day-care chains offer profit-sharing options as part of their benefits package.

RELATED JOBS

- Education director
- School administrator
- Small business owner

GATHERING MORE FACTS

National Association for the Education of Young Children
1509 Sixteenth Street, NW
Washington, DC 20036
Internet: www.naeyc.org

National Association of Child Care Professionals
P.O. Box 90723
Austin, TX 78709-0723
Phone: (800) 537-1118
Internet: www.naccp.org

National Child Care Association (NCCA)
1016 Rosser Street
Conyers, GA 30012
Phone: (800) 543-7161
Internet: www.nccanet.org

11. *Education Director*

DEFINITION

Education directors plan, develop, and execute educational programs at museums and other similar cultural institutions.

TRANSFERABLE TEACHING SKILLS

- Motivating people
- Active listening
- Social perceptiveness

NECESSARY SKILLS

- Strong communication skills
- Flexibility and organizing skills
- Ability to teach and motivate people of all ages

SUCCESS TIPS

- Be aware of others' reactions
- Identify the key causes of behavior
- Adjust your actions to others' actions

9 TO 5: HOW YOU WILL SPEND YOUR DAY

Education directors carry out the educational goals of zoos, museums, botanical gardens, and other similar institutions. They plan courses or schedules that are offered by their museum or zoo. They may even employ educational staff members or lecturers from local colleges to head tours or discussion groups. Education directors are normally responsible for training staff members and may work with university faculty to decide on the content of a class or lecture. They also prepare course outlines and help to establish necessary criteria for those selected to teach the classes.

Education directors sometimes promote their programs in newspapers and on local radio and television. They may meet with school or community groups about their program offerings. The education director is also responsible for the budgets of all educational programs and supervises all records of spending and income. Education directors collaborate with exhibit designers, assisting in the creation of displays that enhance a presentation.

WHERE YOU WILL SPEND YOUR DAY

Most education directors enjoy being in zoos, botanical gardens, museums, or other educational environments. This allows them to interact with scientists, scholars, and researchers. Generally, education directors spend most of their time working in-house.

CAREER FORECAST

Employment opportunities for education directors are expected to increase more slowly than average through the year 2006

From Classroom to . . .

For Karen Stiles, being the *director of education* at a large children's museum keeps her on her toes every minute of the day. Because Karen spent ten years as a high school English teacher, she has great communication skills, which she uses every day when dealing with school corporations from around the state.

"I now direct a staff of adults instead of a room full of high school students. I use leadership skills that I once used in my English classes; however, I now delegate assignments to make sure everything gets done." Karen occasionally has to remind herself that her staff consists of adults and that their opinions are essential in developing a successful team. She continues to influence the lives of students who visit the museum through the many different educational programs presented there.

---

because of a decrease in appropriated funds. Museums, zoos, and other cultural institutions that employ education directors have reduced the size of their education departments.

MONETARY REWARDS

Salaries for education directors vary greatly, depending on the type, size, and location of employment, along with the experience and education of the director. Average starting salaries begin at $23,000. Those with master's degrees earn between $33,000 and $56,000. Fringe benefits depend on employer policies, but usually include retirement plan, sick leave, medical and dental insurance, and paid vacations.

UP THE LADDER

There is not much room for career advancement as an education director. Education directors primarily concentrate on expert familiarity with their institution's valued collection.

Related Jobs

- Archivist
- Librarian
- Museum director

Gathering More Facts

American Association for State and Local History
1717 Church Street
Nashville, TN 37203-2991
Phone: (615) 320-3203
E-mail: history@aaslh.org
Internet: www.aaslh.org

American Association of Botanical Gardens and Arboreta
351 Longwood Road
Kenneth Square, PA 19348
Phone: (610) 925-2500

American Association of Museums
1575 I Street, NW, Suite 400
Washington, DC 20005
Phone: (202) 289-1818
Internet: www.aam-us.org

12. *Bank Manager/Officer*

Definition

Bank managers/officers carry out the policies set forth by the bank's board of directors.

Transferable Teaching Skills

- Leadership
- Communication skills
- Ability to be team player

NECESSARY SKILLS

- Analytical thinking
- Willingness to pursue additional specialized education
- Strong interpersonal skills

SUCCESS TIPS

- Maintain a strong code of ethics
- Have good marketing/sales skills
- Be able to manage employee schedules

9 TO 5: HOW YOU WILL SPEND YOUR DAY

Financial institutions often have a management team in order to carry out their daily operations. All but the smallest banks will have the following managers or officers:

Branch manager, who is responsible for the branch bank's operations

Loan officer, who evaluates the credit worthiness of businesses or individuals who have applied for loans

Operations officer, who plans and implements daily operation procedures

Trust officer, who provides financial counsel, helps people invest funds, and administers trusts or estates

Cashiers, who manage the disbursement and receipt of cash

Bank or branch managers have a solid understanding of how each bank department runs, in order to oversee the daily operations of the branch. The manager's responsibilities vary, according to the size of the branch and the number of management team members. Managers are typically responsible for ordering cash; processing loans; balancing the vault each day; scheduling and supervising tellers; opening new accounts, including checking, savings, trust, and IRA accounts; receiving shipments of cash;

reporting "outages" (cash shortages or overages in transactions); and taking care of customer problems.

Bank managers must constantly promote products and services to the customers. Acquiring new accounts and loans is important to the bank's profitability. Managers must be sure the tellers are up-to-date on new products and services so that they, too, can offer these to customers.

WHERE YOU WILL SPEND YOUR DAY

Bank managers work in comfortable offices and have access to the latest computer systems and information services. Some managers have secretarial support to handle routine clerical duties. Managers commonly work fifty to sixty hours per week and may have to travel to meetings for additional training or to meet customers.

CAREER FORECAST

Individuals with the right skills or experience have the best opportunities in bank management. Strong computer skills, excellent communication skills, and knowledge of international finance will enhance an individual's prospects.

As more banks promote electronic and Internet banking services and open fewer bank branches, management opportunities will become more competitive. Banks may hire temporary managers or contract out for specific needs, increasing the opportunities for "freelancers" in finance.

MONETARY REWARDS

Salaries for bank managers/officers vary, according to the size of the institution. The average annual salary is $55,000. The range of earnings is from a low of $27,600 to a high of $119,000 per year. Benefits usually include insurance, vacations, and retirement pensions. Banks often offer profit sharing and stock ownership opportunities.

UP THE LADDER

Many banks hire for management positions by promoting individuals within the bank. Continuing education is vital for advancement. Managers who gain certification in specialized fields are good candidates for promotion to higher management positions.

RELATED JOBS

- Financial planner
- Real estate adviser
- Insurance consultant

GATHERING MORE FACTS

American Bankers Association
Center for Banking Information
1120 Connecticut Avenue, NW
Washington, DC 20036
Phone: (800) BANKERS
Internet: www.aba.com

Financial Women International
200 Glebe Road, Suite 820
Arlington, VA 22203-3728
Phone: (703) 807-2007
Internet: www.fwi.org

National Bankers Association
1513 P Street, NW
Washington, DC 20009
Phone: (202) 588-5432
Internet: www.natbankers.com

13. *Public Relations Manager*

DEFINITION

Public relations managers oversee public relations staff for organizations or people.

TRANSFERABLE TEACHING SKILLS

- Service-orientation
- Good coordination
- Listening

NECESSARY SKILLS

- Excellent communication skills
- Imagination and enthusiasm
- Charm and reliability

SUCCESS TIPS

- Actively look for ways to help people
- Identify the nature of problems
- Know how to identify essential information

9 TO 5: HOW YOU WILL SPEND YOUR DAY

In today's highly communicative society, public image is one of the most important qualities that people and organizations must develop. If left to their own designs, these entities could easily harm their public image, so they turn to experts in maintaining public favor. These experts are public relations workers. A public relations manager is hired to serve as their representative, coordinator, and supervisor.

In industries, these managers distribute information to stockholders, media, employees, and the general public, particularly when the company's view on an important issue is questioned. The managers also evaluate sales promotion programs from the marketing department to ensure that these do not compromise public relations efforts.

Public relations managers sometimes work to improve the relationship between management and employees. PR managers often publish the company newsletter and file complaints that directly deal with the image of the company.

WHERE YOU WILL SPEND YOUR DAY

Public relations managers typically have pleasant offices located near those of the employer's top executives. These offices serve as the meeting ground for visitors. Work hours are long, with regular business dinners, press luncheons, and late meetings. Travel is often necessary to meet with special interest groups, officials, or clients.

CAREER FORECAST

The various businesses that are only now realizing the importance of public image will ensure that many public relations managers will be needed.

MONETARY REWARDS

Salaries range from $28,000 to $250,000 a year, with an average of $44,000 a year. Earnings typically depend upon experience, location, and the perceived importance of public image. Benefits may include health insurance, tuition payments for education, vacations, and pension plans.

UP THE LADDER

Because of the high visibility of this career, successful depiction of a favorable public image usually means promotion to top executive positions. Training in management skills often ensures promotion.

Related Jobs

- Marketing research analyst
- Promotion specialist
- Sales representative

Gathering More Facts

International Association of Business Communicators
One Hallidie Plaza, Suite 600
San Francisco, CA 94102-2818
Phone: (415) 544-4700
Internet: www.iabc.com

National School Public Relations Association
15948 Derwood Road
Rockville, MD 20855
Phone: (301) 519-0496
Internet: www.nspra.org

Public Relations Society of America
33 Irving Place, Third Floor
New York, NY 10003-2376
Phone: (212) 995-2230
Internet: www.prsa.org

14. *Sales Manager*

Definition

Sales managers train and supervise sales staff members within a company.

Transferable Teaching Skills

- Service orientation
- Monitoring
- Visioning

Necessary Skills

- Good mathematical skills
- Good communication
- Marketing

Success Tips

- Develop approaches for implementing an idea
- Have knowledge of ways to help people
- Be able to persuade others

9 to 5: How You Will Spend Your Day

The sales department of every company is one of its hinges. Any company without a successful sales department will go bankrupt, regardless of the demand for its product. Sales managers ensure that a company's sales department becomes and remains successful. They are generally responsible for the hiring, training, and actions of every sales staff member, although their specific duties vary from company to company.

Managers establish territories, goals, and quotas for each of their departments' workers. These goals are determined after sales managers apply market analysis techniques to determine customer demands and needs, sales volumes potential, and pricing schedules. These goals are accompanied by carefully developed sales campaigns. Managers assign sales territories, or graphic regions, to each of the sales staff members.

Managers are responsible for the conduct of their staff members, thus regularly evaluate them to ensure that they meet expectations. Managers represent their companies at trade association conventions and product promotion meetings. Some sales managers are responsible for product research and development; others only recommend or approve budgets for product research and development.

WHERE YOU WILL SPEND YOUR DAY

Sales managers may be found working in pleasant offices, but they are just as likely to be out in the field training, directing, or evaluating sales staff. Work hours are long and irregular, with frequent evening and weekend meetings with other executives.

CAREER FORECAST

Many companies emphasize the hiring of sales staff rather than sales managers. Therefore, growth of this field may be slow.

MONETARY REWARDS

Salaries range from $25,000 to $250,000 a year, depending upon the company's size and the manager's experience. Benefits may include vacations, health insurance, life insurance, retirement plans, and possibly even company stock options.

UP THE LADDER

Sales managers have little advancement ahead of them, although they can transfer to jobs that are more satisfying, monetarily or otherwise. Some managers are fortunate enough to be promoted to their company's vice-presidential or presidential position.

RELATED JOBS

- Buyer
- Real estate agent
- Securities sales worker

GATHERING MORE FACTS

American Management Association
1601 Broadway
New York, NY 10019-7420

Phone: (212) 586-8100
Internet: www.amanet.org

Sales and Marketing Executive, International
5500 Interstate North Parkway, NW, Suite 545
Atlanta, GA 30328-4662
Internet: www.smei.org

15. *School Administrator*

DEFINITION

School administrators oversee all aspects of daily school functions.

TRANSFERABLE TEACHING SKILLS

- Supervising
- Budgeting
- Problem-solving

NECESSARY SKILLS

- Interpersonal skills
- Ability to communicate well
- Ability to motivate others

SUCCESS TIPS

- Get teams to work together
- Think quickly
- Counsel wisely

9 TO 5: HOW YOU WILL SPEND YOUR DAY

School administrators operate on several levels: as federal and state school administrators, as superintendents, and as school principals. Federal and state government agencies employ school administrators to work in governmental departments of education. Federal administrators create academic standards and programs and distribute money to schools. State administrators interpret state policy, which determines teaching standards, student transportation, and school lunches. School superintendents govern school districts composed of several schools. They execute the school board's decision on hiring practices, curriculum, and budget. They are responsible for establishing and maintaining productive communication with students and parents and keeping up the physical maintenance of the school. As with superintendents, principals are considered representatives of their respective schools. They also serve as liaisons between the community and their school.

WHERE YOU WILL SPEND YOUR DAY

School administrators normally work long hours and are on call in case of emergency. Superintendents have to spend extra time traveling and attending meetings. Principals must attend special after-school functions, such as sporting events and concerts. All in all, the job can be prestigious but also demanding.

CAREER FORECAST

Not much growth is expected for this field in the next few years. As school systems are restructured and downsizing becomes more of a trend with administrative occupations, available administrative positions in education will become scarce. Competition will be tough for the few available jobs.

MONETARY REWARDS

Experience and education determine earnings for school administrators. Principals currently earn an average of $67,400 annually. Superintendents average about $70,000 annually. Health insurance, pension plans, and paid holidays and vacations of two to four weeks are benefits that school administrators can also expect.

Up the Ladder

School principals with experience and success could move on to become school superintendents. School superintendents can eventually accept more challenging positions with larger districts.

Related Jobs

- Library director
- Recreation and park manager
- Social service agency administrator

Gathering More Facts

American Association of School Administrators
1801 North Moore Street
Arlington, VA 22209-1813
Phone (703) 528-0700
Internet: www.aasa.org

From Classroom to ...

Paul Davis is an *elementary school principal*. He started his career as a sixth-grade teacher.

"I became interested in administration when I was asked to be the 'acting principal' of the school when the principal took an extended medical leave.

"Being an elementary principal can be demanding, but it is fun, exciting, and every day is different."

Paul often works from 7 A.M. until 5:30 P.M. and may even stay later if the school has events such as ball games, parent-teacher meetings, or committee meetings.

"Although I have seen several principal colleagues advance to higher administrative positions such as superintendent, I am very satisfied continuing to lead my elementary school."

National Association of Elementary School Principals
1615 Duke Street, Alexandria, VA 22314
Phone: (800) 38-NAESP [(800) 386-2377]
Internet: www.naesp.org/

National Association of Secondary School Principals
1904 Association Drive
Reston, VA 20191-1537
Phone: (703) 860-0200
Internet: www.nassp.org

16. *Retail Sales Manager*

DEFINITION

Retail sales managers supervise employees and store operations to ensure that their stores make a profit.

TRANSFERABLE TEACHING SKILLS

- Time management
- Monitoring
- Operations analysis

NECESSARY SKILLS

- Excellent communication
- Strong interpersonal
- Patience and attentiveness to detail

SUCCESS TIPS

- Be able to assess product sales
- Manage employee scheduling
- Identify and solve problems

9 TO 5: HOW YOU WILL SPEND YOUR DAY

General merchandise stores, such as department stores, and specialty stores, such as sporting goods outlets, hire retail sales managers to ensure that they maintain healthy levels of profit and sales. Retail sales managers' duties depend largely upon the size of the store. The store's operations are in four divisions: merchandising or purchasing and sales; management, which is personnel maintenance and shipping and receiving; accounting; and advertising. In small stores, managers must perform tasks in all four areas. A manager in a large store might only develop and distribute policies to the department heads of each division. Some very large independent stores might have a management team rather than a single sales manager. Such a team usually is made up of a store manager, a manager of operations, a controller, and a manager of advertising.

A specialized type of store manager is the fashion coordinator, employed by some large independent department stores. Fashion coordinators work under merchandise managers and serve as advisers to managers and buyers, to ensure that all of the clothing departments contain the same fashions. Fashion coordinators also develop and supervise store fashion shows, as they are often former models with retailing experience.

WHERE YOU WILL SPEND YOUR DAY

Retail sales managers spend most of their time roaming around their stores, ensuring that all is running smoothly. Managers also have pleasant offices, in which they handle secretarial and administrative duties. Retail managers work about fifty hours a week. Managers in chain operations are likely to be relocated to other stores.

CAREER FORECAST

The future growth of retailing ensures that this field will grow as well.

MONETARY REWARDS

Earnings depend upon experience and sales volume, but salaries typically range from $18,400 to $47,000 a year. The salaries of many managers are supplemented by performance-based bonuses or profit-sharing plans. Benefits include vacations, life insurance, health insurance, and pension plans.

UP THE LADDER

Advancement requires experience and success. Retail managers typically advance to other management positions or to the manager position of another, more desirable store. Some retail sales managers have the opportunity to advance to executive positions.

RELATED JOBS

* Bank manager
* Health services administrator
* Hotel manager

GATHERING MORE FACTS

National Retail Federation
325 7th Street, NW, Suite 1100
Washington, DC 20004-2608
Phone: (202) 783-7971
Internet: www.nrf.com

North American Retail Dealers Association
10 East 22nd Street, Suite 310
Lombard, IL 60148-6191
Phone: (800) 621-0298
Internet: www.narda.com

National Association of Convenience Stores
1605 King Street
Alexandria, VA 22314-2792

From Classroom to . . .

Mary Carnes taught middle school math for fourteen years before deciding to pursue a career in *retail management*. "I worked in retail while I was going to college. Managing a store has many similarities to running a classroom. I have to be well organized, be patient with my employees, and consistently encourage them through positive reinforcement."

Mary spends some of her time training, monitoring, and evaluating her staff. "I issue quarterly evaluations that are very much like giving out report cards to middle schoolers."

Phone: (703) 684-3600
Internet: www.cstorecentral.com

17. *Zoo and Aquarium Director*

DEFINITION

Zoo and aquarium directors direct and supervise the affairs of zoos and aquariums.

TRANSFERABLE TEACHING SKILLS

- Budgeting
- Developing
- Inspecting

NECESSARY SKILLS

- Good communication
- Excellent leadership and people skills
- Excellent time-management

SUCCESS TIPS

- Love animals
- Schedule effectively
- Be able to implement your ideas

9 TO 5: HOW YOU WILL SPEND YOUR DAY

Zoos and aquariums no longer focus purely on entertainment, as they did years ago. Now their primary objectives are public education and wildlife preservation. The responsibilities, therefore, of zoo and aquarium directors have shifted from day-to-day concerns to long-term objectives that require greater administrative skill. Directors operate under the guidance of a volunteer governing board.

Directors are most concerned with the finances of their institutions. Zoo and aquarium financial resources include government tax money, donations, membership fees, retail sales, and visitor services. From the money obtained through these sources, directors must plan overall budgets for animal acquisitions, research projects, public education, and so on.

Directors must oversee renovation efforts to ensure that facilities are improved with a conservation image. Directors are responsible for informing the public about events, often through on-site speeches or television and radio messages. Directors are the visible representatives of their institutions. As such, they usually take an active part in conservation efforts and conservation organization committee actions.

WHERE YOU WILL SPEND YOUR DAY

Directors spend a lot of time in on-site offices, handling business administration matters. Travel is sometimes necessary to conferences, events, and meetings, particularly if a director is heavily involved in conservation. Work hours are long, and nearly every director takes work home each night.

CAREER FORECAST

The slow growth of new zoos severely limits opportunities in this field. Prospects are about the same for aquarium directors.

MONETARY REWARDS

Salaries range from $28,000 to more than $100,000 a year, depending upon the size of the institution. Benefits are excellent, including medical insurance, vacations, and retirement plans. Private corporate institutions may offer profit sharing as well.

UP THE LADDER

Advancement is generally rare. Some directors may move to a larger facility or to an entirely different field in search of advancement. Directors are at the top of their ladders.

RELATED JOBS

- College/university administrator
- Library director
- Museum curator/archivist

From Classroom to . . .

"The administrative experience I gained as a principal has been very helpful in my position as a zoo director. Supervising staff, planning education and conservation projects, and serving as the zoo's spokesperson come easily to me because of my past work experience. My professional contacts in the education field are helpful when I need to promote the zoo or need support in funding campaigns."

—HEATHER THOMAS, *zoo director*

Gathering More Facts

American Association of Museums
1575 I Street, NW, Suite 400
Washington, DC 20005
Phone: (202) 289-1818
Internet: www.aam-us.org

American Association of Zoo Keepers, Inc.
Topeka Zoological Park
635 Southwest Gage Boulevard
Topeka, KS 66606-1980
Phone: (785) 273-1980
Internet: www.aazk.ind.net

American Zoo and Aquarium Association
Conservation Center
7970-D Old Georgetown Road
Bethesda, MD 20814-2493
Internet: www.aza.org

18. College/University Administrator

Definition

College/University administrators develop, maintain, and oversee college and university programs.

Transferable Teaching Skills

- Overseeing
- Implementation planning
- Time management

Necessary Skills

- Master's degree in an administrative field
- Strong organizational and managerial skills
- Efficiency and decisiveness

Success Tips

- Be computer literate
- Acquire financial experience
- Maintain good community relations

9 to 5: How You Will Spend Your Day

Administrators have a variety of responsibilities, depending upon the areas overseen. The president oversees all administrators and the operation of the campus. The provost oversees actual academics, such as faculty and curricular concerns. Admissions directors oversee admission procedures, student files, and application procedures. Financial aid directors manage student financial assistance programs. Registrars oversee class scheduling and student transcripts. The dean of students oversees student affairs, such as extracurricular activities, housing, and counseling.

Where You Will Spend Your Day

These administrators typically work in large, comfortable offices. Usually, they work throughout the entire year, with their longest hours during the beginning and end of each term. Some must work at night, on weekends, or both, while some must travel to complete their duties.

Career Forecast

Job availability depends upon the enrollment and finances of schools, but it is slow overall because most positions are filled.

Monetary Rewards

Salaries range from $36,800 to $80,000 a year, depending upon school size and job responsibilities. Full benefits are usually part of the salary package.

Up the Ladder

Assistants advance through specialization or relocation to a larger school.

Related Jobs

- Social services administrator
- Professional organization manager
- Library director

Gathering More Facts

American Association of University Administrators
P.O. Box 696
Heflin, AL 36264-0696
Phone: (205) 758-2682

College and University Personnel Association
1233 20th Street, NW, Suite 301
Washington, DC 20036-1250
Phone: (202) 429-0311
Internet: www.cupa.org

National Association for College Admission Counseling
1631 Prince Street
Alexandria, VA 22314
Phone: (800) 822-6285
Internet: www.nacac.com

The Business World

Opportunities in the business field should be excellent over the next ten years. The best opportunities will be found in small businesses. As you begin to search for a job in the business world, look closely at new and growing businesses that provide products and services focusing on the future economy.

Many job opportunities exist for teachers making a career change into the business world. Jobs that tap into the creativeness and instructional abilities of teachers can be found in abundant supply. This chapter explores just a few of those career ideas.

19. Advertising/Marketing Consultant

DEFINITION

Advertising/marketing consultants advise individuals, small businesses, and large corporations about market trends to predict advertising outcomes.

TRANSFERABLE TEACHING SKILLS

- Solid writing skills
- Ability to develop ideas
- Ability to explain new ideas

Necessary Skills

- Creative thinking
- Persuading
- Marketing

Success Tips

- Be familiar with basic design terms and processes
- Communicate well
- Publicize effectively

9 to 5: How You Will Spend Your Day

Typical advertising/marketing consultants do one of two things; they either fulfill a role in a business's everyday staff or they are freelancers who work with smaller businesses unable to afford a full-time consultant. Their role is to properly evaluate market potential for current trends, the survivability of products, and the effectiveness of advertising campaigns.

Advertising/marketing consultants must mold themselves to a variety of client needs, particularly if they are freelance consultants. Full-service consultants must be able to conceptualize, design, and execute complete marketing campaigns. Consultants of a lower expertise level will be restricted to fulfilling any part of a campaign and then delegating out the remainder of the work to freelancers. Projects may be as simple as wedding invitation designs or as complex as extensive advertising campaigns for international corporations.

Where You Will Spend Your Day

Most consultants work either in office space provided by an employer or in self-owned office space. Freelancers often work in a home environment. Home-based consultants either market their services through the Internet or else travel to employing businesses to determine those companies' needs.

CAREER FORECAST

Advertising/marketing consultants tend to be extremely competitive, as campaigns must constantly be restructured to accommodate consumer demands; therefore, a high turnover rate exists for these consultants, particularly for freelancers.

MONETARY REWARDS

Hourly rates range from $30 to $100 for freelancers, while any consultant can earn from $30,000 to $100,000 a year.

UP THE LADDER

Advancement depends almost solely on the consultant's ability to predict what will attract consumer attention to clients' products. Success equals higher pay and more contracts for freelancers, and it equals higher pay and better benefits for salaried consultants.

RELATED JOBS

- Sales
- Regional planner
- Sociologist

GATHERING MORE FACTS

American Advertising Federation
Education Services Department
1101 Vermont Avenue, NW, Suite 500
Washington, DC 20005-6306
Phone: (202) 898-0089
Internet: www.aaf.org

Marketing Research Association
1344 Silas Deane Highway, Suite 306
Rocky Hill, CT 06067-0230
Internet: www.mra-net.org

National Association for Business Economics
1233 20th Street, NW, Suite 505
Washington, DC 20036
Internet: www.nabe.com

20. *Personnel and Labor Relations Specialist*

DEFINITION

Personnel and labor relations specialists serve as formulators of personnel policy and as mediators between employers and employees.

TRANSFERABLE TEACHING SKILLS

- Good interpersonal skills
- Ability to verbalize information clearly
- Ability to implement your ideas

NECESSARY SKILLS

- Analyzing
- Overseeing
- Investigating

SUCCESS TIPS

- Be able to discuss negative issues in a nonoffending way
- Express policies effectively
- Create a harmonious working environment

9 TO 5: HOW YOU WILL SPEND YOUR DAY

Personnel and labor relations specialists ensure that management uses employees wherever they will be most effective.

These specialists also ensure that employees find fulfillment in their jobs and working conditions. They interview potential workers, select or recommend future workers, and develop wage, benefits, and training programs.

Personnel clerks handle routine clerical tasks, such as file maintenance and statistical compilation. Personnel managers oversee the personnel departments of large organizations. Industrial relations directors develop personnel policies. Personnel recruiters find and hire or recommend new employees, while employment interviewers filter job applicants to select the best; both of these specialists must operate according to equal employment opportunities guidelines, as sometimes outlined by job development specialists. Job analysts formulate analytical reports on their organizations' jobs to provide employment, training, and wage guidelines. Occupational analysts analyze occupational trends to determine how to more effectively use the workforce. Compensation managers oversee pay systems, while benefits managers oversee benefits programs.

Various types of personnel and labor relations specialists mediate between employers and employees. However, the personnel department occupied by these specialists may consist of only one person for a small business or over fifty people for a complex corporation.

WHERE YOU WILL SPEND YOUR DAY

Personnel and labor relations specialists work in pleasant offices. Occasional travel may be required for meetings or negotiations. Work hours are usually only 35 to 40 hours a week, although businesses with weekend hours may desire these specialists to be present on weekends as well.

CAREER FORECAST

Although this career field should grow over the next few years, an overabundance of qualified applicants will create heavy competition for a limited number of opportunities.

Monetary Rewards

Salaries vary, depending upon business size, location of the business, and the individual's experiences and qualifications. Because of this, earnings range from $19,500 a year for entry-level specialists to $106,100 a year for industrial relations directors. Benefits also vary widely, depending upon the size of the business and the position of the specialists.

Up the Ladder

Trainee specialists are given basic tasks, then are assigned to specific areas for specialized training. Advancement consists of promotion to supervisory positions, but these are obtained only with advanced education and experience.

Related Jobs

- Career and employment counselor and technician
- Human resource specialist
- Management analyst and consultant

Gathering More Facts

American Society for Training and Development
1640 King Street, Box 1443
Alexandria, VA 22313-2043
Phone: (703) 683-8100
Internet: www.astd.org

Industrial Relations Research Association
121 Labor and Industrial Relations
University of Illinois
504 East Armory, MC-504
Champaign, IL 61820
Phone: (217) 333-0072
Internet: www.irra.uiuc.edu

Professional Association for Compensation, Benefits,
and Total Rewards
14040 Northsight Boulevard
Scottsdale, AZ 85260
Phone: (480) 951-9191
Internet: www.worldatwork.org

21. *Executive Search Recruiter*

DEFINITION

Executive search recruiters are hired by companies to fill senior
management positions with the best people available.

TRANSFERABLE TEACHING SKILLS

- Investigating
- Evaluating
- Discovering

NECESSARY SKILLS

- Networking abilities
- Discretion
- Excellent communication

SUCCESS TIPS

- Cultivate good people skills
- Be organized
- Interview skillfully

9 TO 5: HOW YOU WILL SPEND YOUR DAY

When senior management positions become available within
companies, these can't always be filled from the lower ranks of
management. In these situations, executive search recruiting firms
are often hired. The executive search recruiter for the client gets
complete job descriptions from the personnel director. These

descriptions usually include the necessary skills. The recruiter may have to visit the client company to gain a firm grasp of the company's needs and to make suggestions about these.

An executive search recruiter takes this information and searches through the firm's computer files for resumes of people who match the client's specifications. Anyone who fits the client's needs is then contacted about the position. If no one in the firm's files matches the client's requirements, recruiters search for people working in similar positions in other companies, in order to attract them to the client company's open position.

However they are found, candidates are interviewed over the telephone. Recruiters send written reports on these candidates to the client company, which then directly interviews and selects whomever it desires. Once a candidate is selected and accepts the job, the executive search recruiter is finished.

WHERE YOU WILL SPEND YOUR DAY

Executive search recruiters work in pleasant offices with regular business hours. Travel is often necessary, to ascertain directly a client's needs and to interview candidates. A large portion of recruiters' time is spent on the telephone with clients and candidates.

CAREER FORECAST

This career is growing somewhat rapidly because of the steady increase in newly created senior management positions.

MONETARY REWARDS

An executive search recruiter is paid according to the number of successfully hired candidates, so earnings vary widely. The recruiter's firm receives a percentage of the candidate's salary and benefits, of which the recruiter receives a portion. Typical earnings range from $30,000 to $60,000 a year, and benefits include health and life insurance, a retirement plan, and paid vacations and holidays.

Up the Ladder

Advancement is usually in the form of greater earnings and more important assignments. Recruiters may gain supervisory positions or become partners in the firm. Some recruiters even begin their own firms.

Related Jobs

- Placement counselor
- Public relation specialist
- Social worker

Gathering More Facts

Association of Executive Search Consultants
500 Fifth Avenue, Suite 930
New York, NY 10110
Phone: (212) 398-9556
Internet: www.aesc.org

National Association of Executive Recruiters
20 North Wacker Drive, Suite 2262
Chicago, IL 60606
Phone: (312) 701-0744

National Organization of Executives Recruiters
222 South Westmore Drive, Suite 110
P.O. Box 2156
Altamonte Springs, FL 32715-2156

22. *Financial Planner*

Definition

Financial planners review clients' financial situations and then make suggestions on how to specifically achieve financial goals.

Transferable Teaching Skills

- Estimating
- Budgeting
- Counseling

Necessary Skills

- Ethical character
- Financial knowledge
- Excellent communication skills

Success Tips

- Keep up with continuing financial education
- Have a strong educational and ethical background
- Listen to the clients' needs

9 to 5: How You Will Spend Your Day

Various types of financial assistants exist, such as insurance agents, accountants, and stockbrokers, but most have specialized in a particular aspect of finances. Financial planners take a broad approach to clients' financial situations and advise clients on their overall situations.

Before advising their clients, financial planners gather all financial information from clients' records and other financial advisers. After determining their clients' financial objectives and reviewing the research, financial planners generate reports stating their recommendations, their clients' goals, and all pertinent financial information. These reports must be periodically reviewed and evaluated to determine if any changes are necessary. Financial planners must be prepared to support and explain every aspect of their reports.

Certain goals occupy most of the financial planner's time: tax planning, investment planning, estate planning, retirement planning, and risk management. Whatever goals their clients pursue, financial planners must plan toward these goals in order to build a client base. Telephone solicitation, public seminars, social networking, and referrals all help financial planners build a client base.

Where You Will Spend Your Day

Financial planners usually work in offices, either with or without other financial planners, or at home. Travel is limited to attending civic functions and visiting clients. Hours are usually regular business hours, although beginning planners may work overtime to attract clients or work at night or on weekends to accommodate clients' schedules.

Career Forecast

Because of our nation's increasing affluence and reliance on individual investments, this field should grow quite rapidly.

Monetary Rewards

Through various combinations of consultation fees, commissions, or both, their salaries range from $50,000 to $200,000 or more a year. Those financial planners who work for a firm may receive a minimum salary based on commissions they can be expected to earn. They may also earn vacation days, sick days, and health insurance, but independent financial planners must provide their own benefits.

Up the Ladder

Successful financial planners advance through clientele growth, larger accounts, and years of experience. Some financial planners, once they have achieved success, choose to pursue other financial careers, such as investment banking.

Related Jobs

- Insurance agent
- Real estate agent
- Credit analyst

From Classroom to …

Kevin Smith always enjoyed teaching, but he wanted a change. Three years ago he decided to leave his junior high math classroom and become a *financial planner.* Kevin was selected because he had good personal qualities and the skills necessary for excellent customer service. He says, "The company provided me with the additional training I would need to get started. I really feel that the good interpersonal and communication skills that I learned in my educational classes helped me be selected for this job."

Kevin feels that this is a great career for a teacher about to leave the classroom because many people have transferred from other jobs who now use their skills to help people plan for a more secure financial future.

GATHERING MORE FACTS

Certified Financial Planner Board of Standards
1700 Broadway, Suite 2100
Denver, CO 80290-2101
Phone: (303) 830-7500
Internet: www.cfp-board.org

College of Financial Planning
6161 South Syracuse Way
Greenwood Village, CO 80111-4707
Phone: (303) 220-1200
Internet: www.fp.edu

National Association of Personal Financial Advisors
355 West Dundee Road, Suite 200
Buffalo Grove, IL 60089
Phone: (888) 333-6659
Internet: www.napfa.org

23. *Insurance Claims Representative*

DEFINITION

Insurance claims representatives, or claims adjusters, determine the liability of insurance companies and try to arrange out-of-court settlements with legitimate claimants.

TRANSFERABLE TEACHING SKILLS

- Estimating
- Investigating
- Computing

NECESSARY SKILLS

- Good memory skills
- Knowledge of computer applications
- Strong communication skills

SUCCESS TIPS

- Stay abreast of insurance laws and regulations
- Have a good eye for detail
- Be accurate at estimating repair or replacement costs

9 TO 5: HOW YOU WILL SPEND YOUR DAY

Because of the prevalence and ease with which false insurance claims are made and because accurate estimates and settlements must be made on legitimate claims, insurance companies need insurance claims representatives to investigate and make judgments on claims. Some of these people are called claims clerks, who evaluate every insurance form to ensure that all pertinent information has been filled in. Claims clerks then place this information in a claim file and evaluate the amount of coverage given in the policy.

Routine claims, such as minor accidents, are usually quickly settled with minimal investigation, but some claims may require extensive investigation on the part of a claims adjuster. After a claims adjuster examines the physical evidence, reports, and testimonies of all witnesses (such as the claimant, bystanders, police, and hospital personnel), a settlement is usually negotiated. Suspected false claims are reported to higher authorities.

Claims adjusters usually specialize in a particular type of insurance investigation, such as fire or automobile insurance. Inside or telephone adjusters handle minor and routine claims, often by telephone, while outside adjusters actually investigate claims in the field.

WHERE YOU WILL SPEND YOUR DAY

Inside claims adjusters and clerks work in well-lit offices for 35 to 40 hours a week, with occasional overtime during peak claim periods and quarterly reports. Outside claims adjusters travel extensively, with irregular hours. All insurance claims representatives may be on call 24 hours a day.

CAREER FORECAST

Because of the increase in insurance sales in our affluent society, this career looks quite promising for the next few years.

MONETARY REWARDS

Claims adjusters have an average salary of $22,800 a year, with supervisory positions paying as much as $55,000 a year. Business travel receives reimbursements, and fringe benefits are strong, with liberal vacation policies and retirement programs.

UP THE LADDER

Advancement opportunities are plentiful for those who show competent success. Greater responsibilities and even supervisory positions are available as advancement.

Related Jobs

- Accountant
- Insurance underwriter
- Risk manager

Gathering More Facts

Insurance Information Institute
110 William Street
New York, NY 10038
Phone: (212) 346-5500
Internet: www.iii.org

Insurance Institute of America
720 Providence Road
P.O. Box 3016
Malvern, PA 19355-0716
Phone: (610) 644-2100
Internet: www.aicpcu.org

Life Office Management Association
2300 Windy Ridge Parkway, Suite 600
Atlanta, GA 30327-4308
Phone: (770) 984-6434
Internet: www.loma.org/intl-hp.htm

24. *Insurance Underwriter*

Definition

Insurance underwriters evaluate insurance applications to determine the degree of risk an individual presents, determine premium rates, and write policies.

Transferable Teaching Skills

- Ability to make difficult decisions
- Good written skills
- Ability to explain yourself

Necessary Skills

- Analytical thinking
- Logical thinking
- Ability to be detail-oriented

Success Tips

- Enjoy writing
- Have an eye for detail
- Practice good organizational skills

9 to 5: How You Will Spend Your Day

Billions of dollars in risks are assumed by insurance companies each year from the shoulders of insurance policy holders. Insurance underwriters are responsible for ensuring that their companies do not assume too much or too severe of a risk in issuing insurance to an individual. Underwriters are required to meticulously analyze insurance applications and all pertinent accompanying information, such as medical reports, loss control specialist reports, and actuarial studies.

From these analyses, insurance underwriters determine the premium that the company is prepared to offer an individual. Greater risk assessment by an underwriter equals a greater premium quoted to that individual. The success of an insurance company depends upon its underwriters. Conservative evaluations lead to higher premium quotes, which lose business to more liberal companies, while liberal evaluations lead to low premium quotes, which can cause companies to lose money as they cover greater risks. Therefore, insurance underwriters must walk a fine line in risk evaluation, often achieved by specializing in one type of insurance.

Where You Will Spend Your Day

Insurance underwriters almost always work in a pleasant office environment. Travel is rare, but meetings or classes may be attended in other cities. Work hours are usually typical business hours, 35 to 40 hours a week, but overtime is an occasional option.

Career Forecast

Although the growth of the public's security consciousness may create a demand for insurance underwriters, the increased use of risk assessment software has greatly slowed the growth of this career for now.

Monetary Rewards

Insurance underwriters earn from $24,000 to $50,000 a year, with supervisory positions paying $60,000 or more a year. Benefits are nearly always good for insurance company employees, including liberal vacation allotments and retirement plans.

Up the Ladder

Continuing education is the key to advancing as an insurance underwriter. This, along with proven leadership abilities, results in underwriters being promoted to supervisory positions.

Related Jobs

- Auditor
- Actuary
- Risk manager

Gathering More Facts

American Society of Chartered Life Underwriters
270 South Bryn Mawr Avenue
Bryn Mawr, PA 19010-2195
Phone: (610) 526-2500

Insurance Information Institute
110 William Street
New York, NY 10038
Phone: (212) 346-5500
Internet: www.iii.org

Insurance Institute of America
720 Providence Road
P.O. Box 3016
Malvern, PA 19355-0716
Phone: (610) 644-2100
Internet: www.aicpcu.org

25. *Buyer*

DEFINITION

Buyers purchase merchandise from manufacturers or whole-salers and resell this merchandise to retailers, institutions, and the general public.

TRANSFERABLE TEACHING SKILLS

- Overseeing
- Classifying
- Delivering

NECESSARY SKILLS

- Integrity
- Analytical judgment
- Inspecting ability

SUCCESS TIPS

- Have knowledge of the retail market
- Be able to determine correct quantity of needed supplies
- Be able to estimate profit

9 TO 5: HOW YOU WILL SPEND YOUR DAY

The economic system of production, distribution, and merchandising is so complex that two types of buyers exist—wholesale buyers and retail buyers. Wholesale buyers purchase goods from manufacturers and resell them in smaller quantities to retailers and other commercial institutions. Retail buyers typically purchase merchandise from wholesalers, but they may occasionally purchase goods from manufacturers. Retail buyers purchase these goods for resale to the public.

Specifically, retail buyers work for retail stores, either in a supervisory position beneath a merchandise manager or in a strictly purchasing position. All retail buyers must understand their store's policies, budgets, needs, and trends. All buyers must be experts in the goods they purchase and must order goods months in advance to anticipate buying seasons. Purchasing is done through traveling salespeople with samples and catalogs, suppliers with mail or telephone ordering services, business trips to merchandise showrooms and manufacturing establishments in other cities, or any combination of these methods.

WHERE YOU WILL SPEND YOUR DAY

Pleasant surroundings are usually provided for buyers. Travel, in the form of buying trips, is possible, which may mean being absent from home for a few days each month. Hours are long and irregular, particularly during holidays. Evening and weekend overtime is common.

CAREER FORECAST

The increasing use of computers for purchasing and the centralization of buying in today's stores severely limit the available job opportunities.

MONETARY REWARDS

Earnings depend upon a number of factors, particularly on the extent of the employer's sales. Salaries range from $18,000 a year for beginning retail buyers to $63,000 a year for mass merchandisers buyers. Cash bonuses, profit sharing, stock options, and discounts are often available for successful buyers, in addition to the usual benefits.

Up the Ladder

Advancement is achieved through success and reliability under pressure. Buyers typically may advance to supervisory positions within their merchandising departments, and those with the most experience may even be able to advance to top executive positions in larger retail chains.

Related Jobs

- Sales manager
- Insurance sales agent
- Service sales representative

Gathering More Facts

American Purchasing Society
430 West Downer Place
Aurora, IL 60506
Phone: (630) 859-0250
Internet: www.american-purchasing.com

National Association of Purchasing Management
P.O. Box 22160
Tempe, AZ 85285-2160
Phone: (800) 888-6276
Internet: www.napm.org

National Institute of Government Purchasing, Inc.
11800 Sunrise Valley Drive, Suite 1050
Reston, VA 20191-53002
Phone: (730) 715-9400
Internet: http://nigp.org

26. *Purchasing Agent*

DEFINITION

Purchasing agents purchase raw materials, goods, and services for the operations of their companies.

TRANSFERABLE TEACHING SKILLS

- Overseeing
- Processing
- Supervising

NECESSARY SKILLS

- Auditing
- Projecting
- Reporting

SUCCESS TIPS

- Be a problem solver
- Pay extraordinary attention to detail
- Coordinate many activities at once

9 TO 5: HOW YOU WILL SPEND YOUR DAY

Retail and wholesale buyers purchase goods for resale by their companies, while purchasing agents buy raw materials and supplies to keep their companies in business. Companies that employ purchasing agents include manufacturers, schools, hospitals, government offices, and other businesses. All of these companies employ purchasing agents to ensure having enough supplies to continue smooth operation. These purchases must be the best in quality for their intended uses; a purchase whose quality is too high is a waste of money, whereas too low is also costly because the product may not last very long.

Purchasing agents must also consider quantity, timing of the purchase, and pricing. Pricing includes not only the cost of the goods or services, but handling, transportation, and unloading costs as well. Costs often vary according to season. Timing is important because of this price variance and also because production must not be slowed by material shortage.

Purchasing agents must anticipate supplier schedules, including potential delivery problems or production stoppage, in order to continue supplying the company with the necessary goods for production. Agents get their information from price lists, sales representatives, and supplier showrooms or plants.

Where You Will Spend Your Day

Purchasing agents work in pleasant office environments. Travel is rare; occasionally, agents must visit suppliers and attend company conferences. They work about 35 to 40 hours a week, although overtime may occasionally be necessary, particularly in seasonal industries.

Career Forecast

Because of the computerization of inventories, the growth of this career will be minimal; few openings will exist in the future.

Monetary Rewards

A purchasing agent's salary is typically about $33,000 a year, although it may be as much as $60,000 a year for supervisory positions. Purchasing agents may receive bonuses, depending upon the business and its yearly profits. Benefits usually include paid holidays, vacations, pension plans, and health insurance.

Up the Ladder

Advanced education and experience are usually the keys to promotion to supervisory positions. Purchasing agents may advance to the position of department head of purchasing, traffic, or warehousing departments.

RELATED JOBS

- Wholesale sales representative
- Marketing and advertising manager
- Service sales representative

GATHERING MORE FACTS

American Purchasing Society
430 West Downer Place
Aurora, IL 60506
Phone: (630) 859-0250
Internet: www.american-purchasing.com

Federal Acquisition Institute (MVI)
Office of Acquisition Policy
General Service Administration
1800 F Street, NW, Room 4017
Washington, DC 20405
Internet: gsa.gov/staff/v/training.htm

National Association of Purchasing Management
2055 East Centennial Circle
P.O. Box 22160
Tempe, AZ 85285-2160
Phone: (480) 752-6276, (800) 888-6276
Internet: www.napm.org

27. *Insurance Agent*

DEFINITION

Insurance agents sell insurance policies to businesses and individuals, offering protection against financial loss.

Transferable Teaching Skills

- Estimating
- Interviewing
- Calculating

Necessary Skills

- Ability to communicate effectively
- Confidence
- Mathematical skill

Success Tips

- Enjoy working outside an office
- Understand the state and federal insurance and tax laws
- Observe and weigh the aspects of each case

9 to 5: How You Will Spend Your Day

Insurance agents assist families and businesses select insurance policies that offer the best protection of life, health, business, furniture, vehicles, jewelry, personal valuables, and other properties. Insurance agents maintain records and prepare reports

---

From Classroom to ...

"As a teacher, I was outgoing and enthusiastic. Those qualities have been the backbone of my success as an insurance agent. The skills I learned during my teaching career, such as being a careful listener and an effective communicator, inspire confidence from my clients. As a teacher, I met many people who became the base for my insurance career contacts."

—Kelli Roberson, *insurance agent*

for clients. If there is a loss, agents assist policyholders in settling their insurance claims. Some agents assist employers in providing insurance through payroll deductions to employees.

Insurance agents may sell one or several types of insurance, such as health, life, disability, property and casualty, and long-term care insurance. More insurance agents are providing comprehensive financial planning services, such as retirement planning counseling, to clients as well. Insurance agents also use the Internet to advertise services and describe the types of financial products they offer.

WHERE YOU WILL SPEND YOUR DAY

Insurance agents generally work out of small offices, but most of their time is spent in the field, contacting clients and closing sales. Agents usually establish work hours that are convenient for their clients, which means evenings and weekends. Forty-hour weeks are normal, but some weeks may require sixty hours or more.

CAREER FORECAST

Employment opportunities are not expected to increase. Most job openings occur as a result of agents leaving the field for other occupations. Offering advice on a wide variety of insurance and financial services is the best way to pursue employment. Because of computers, larger volumes of sales can be made with fewer agents.

MONETARY REWARDS

Insurance agents annually earn from $31,500 to $49,000, depending on the employer and geographical location. More experienced agents could earn in excess of $76,900 a year. Most independent agents earn money by commission only. Bonuses are usually earned when profit goals are met for the agency or an agent achieves his or her sales goal.

Up the Ladder

Insurance agents who demonstrate leadership and sales ability can become sales mangers in local offices. Further advancement can lead to promotion to agency superintendent or an executive position. Ultimately, agents can seek to establish their own brokerage firms or independent agencies.

Related Jobs

- Estate planning specialist
- Financial adviser
- Real estate agent

Gathering More Facts

Independent Insurance Agents of America
127 South Peyton Street
Alexandria, VA 22314
Internet: www.iiaa.org

Insurance Information Institute
110 William Street
New York, NY 10038

National Association of Professional Insurance Agents
400 North Washington Street
Alexandria, VA 22314

28. *Real Estate Agent/Broker*

Definition

Real estate agents and brokers execute the intentions of buyers, sellers, or both, of real estate.

TRANSFERABLE TEACHING SKILLS

- Mathematical talent
- People skills
- Time management

NECESSARY SKILLS

- Honesty
- Communication skills
- Ability to organize effectively

SUCCESS TIPS

- Be flexible
- Be patient
- Be able to estimate

9 TO 5: HOW YOU WILL SPEND YOUR DAY

Real estate agents aid clients in their dealings with real estate, whether purchasing, selling, renting, or leasing. The real estate can be any piece of land or property—residential, agricultural, or commercial—with any variety of improvements and buildings on it.

Real estate agents' work begins with obtaining contacts, called listings, for their agencies. This must be done through various methods of solicitation. Once these listings are acquired, agencies' administrators assign real estate agents to them. For each listing, a real estate agent must analyze the property to determine its strongest selling points and its weakest points. Such analysis might result in advising the owner how to improve the property. Often, the agent assigned to a piece of real estate might be asked to appraise the fair market value of the property. Sometimes, buyers might also ask a real estate agent to appraise property.

Once the property is analyzed and appraised, the real estate agent arranges for prospective buyers, also obtained through solicitation, to visit the property. Agents bring together buyers and sellers and oversee their contacts, aiding in financial areas when needed.

WHERE YOU WILL SPEND YOUR DAY

Real estate agents work in pleasant offices or homes, but they are usually found in the field soliciting, analyzing, and appraising real estate. Agents operate on their own work schedules, but tend to take few vacations, as they may miss out on golden opportunities.

CAREER FORECAST

Real estate employment depends largely upon the state of economy, although it should grow very little even during an upswing.

MONETARY REWARDS

Real estate agents earn from $31,000 to $100,000 per year, depending upon the commission rate, which ranges from 5 to 10 percent and averages about 7 percent. Earnings come from commissions on real estate properties. Agents usually have to provide their own benefits.

UP THE LADDER

Many real estate agents advance by expanding the quantity and quality of their work. Others enter management positions in brokerage firms. Some agents advance by specializing in a particular type of real estate, such as commercial or residential.

RELATED JOBS

- Estate manager
- Financial planner
- Personal shopper

GATHERING MORE FACTS

National Association of Realtors
430 North Michigan Avenue
Chicago, IL 60611
Phone: (312) 329-8200
Internet: www.nar.realtor.com

Society of Industrial and Office Realtors
700 11 Street, NW, Suite 50
Washington, DC 2001
Phone: (202) 737-1150
Internet: www.sior.com

The Counselors of Real Estate
430 North Michigan Avenue
Chicago, IL 60611-4089
Phone: (312) 329-8427
Internet: www.cre.org

From Classroom to . . .

Sherry Ford was able to use her past work experience as an elementary school teacher to become a successful *real estate agent.*

"Dealing with parents and children helped me learn patience, compassion, and tact. My clients can be very demanding when they are buying or selling a house."

Sherry loves her job because she is able to meet many people. However, there are downsides to being a real estate agent.

"It's difficult finding time to be with my family and friends. The hours are often irregular and long. There is tremendous pressure to get sales and a lot of rejection associated with selling real estate. Even so, I plan to continue working in real estate for many years to come."

29. *Sales Representative*

DEFINITION

Sales representatives market their company's products to manufacturers, wholesale and retail establishments, government agencies, and other institutions.

TRANSFERABLE TEACHING SKILLS

- Ability to explain new concepts
- Investigating
- Strong interpersonal skills

NECESSARY SKILLS

- Strong education background
- Sales experience
- Confidence

SUCCESS TIPS

- Manifest a desire to sell
- Have an outgoing personality
- Have integrity

9 TO 5: HOW YOU WILL SPEND YOUR DAY

Sales representatives' main objective is to promote their merchandise to clients. Sales representatives must also answer questions or advise clients on how to use the products in their institution or business.

Sales representatives may have samples or catalogs of their products. They inform customers about pricing and availability and help with placing orders. Sales representatives often try to correct problems that customers have with the product.

Competition between sales representatives can be intense. Representatives must explain how their products or services are better than those of competitors. Superior verbal skills can persuade customers to place orders.

Pursuing and securing new accounts are vital to a sales representative's success and possible promotions. The company might set goals or quotas for its sales representatives, requiring them to expand their customer base. In addition to selling products, sales representatives have administrative duties, such as writing reports, making travel plans, filing expense reports, analyzing sales data, and scheduling appointments.

WHERE YOU WILL SPEND YOUR DAY

Sale representatives spent most of their time meeting with current clients or contacting new ones. Sale representatives usually have a sales region or territory that includes several states. They may be required to be on the road for several days or weeks at a time. As a result, sales representatives usually work more than forty hours per week.

CAREER FORECAST

Sale representative job opportunities will be best for those who have technical expertise or extensive knowledge of the product being sold. Small companies will offer more opportunities because they rely more heavily on sales representatives to control costs. Although sales workers will always be needed to demonstrate and sell products, the expected growth in employment opportunities will be slower than average.

MONETARY REWARDS

Earnings vary greatly because employers usually offer a salary along with a commission. Commissions are based on the amount of sales. Some employers offer bonuses for representatives whose performance meets or exceeds company goals or quotas.

The average yearly earnings for sales representative are $36,500. Ambitious representatives can earn more than

$85,000 per year. Benefits can include health and life insurance, pension plans, vacation and sick leave, or a company car.

Up the Ladder

Advancement for sales representatives may involve getting a larger or more valuable sales territory or becoming a sales manager overseeing a team of sales representatives. Some sales representatives go into business for themselves.

Related Jobs

- Insurance agent
- Financial sales agent
- Buyer or purchasing agent

Gathering More Facts

Manufacturers' Agents National Association
P.O. Box 3467
Laguna Hills, CA 92654-3467
Phone: (877) 626-2776
Internet: www.manaonline.org

From Classroom to . . .

How is teaching seventh-grade math like being a *sales representative?* Mike Ables says that both jobs require you to be persuasive: persuading seventh-graders that the math concepts you teach are important and persuading customers that your product can increase their company's profits.

"A successful sales representative is not only persuasive, but also has tact and patience to work with difficult customers. Sales representatives need to be interested in the products they sell, have a neat appearance, and be able to communicate clearly and effectively."

Manufacturers' Representatives Educational Research
    Foundation
P.O. Box 247
Geneva, IL 60134
Phone: (630) 208-1466
Internet: www.mrerf.org

Sales and Manufacturing Executives International
P.O. Box 1390
Sumas, WA 98295-1390
Phone: (312) 893-0751
Internet: www.smei.org

CHAPTER FIVE

Using Communication Skills

As an educator, you're already a natural in the communication business. You talk, and students listen and learn. If you enjoy the communication aspect of teaching, you'll find jobs in this chapter that let you to use verbal skills to earn your salary.

30. Business Plan Writer

DEFINITION

Business plan writers organize the specific details of clients' general business goals.

TRANSFERABLE TEACHING SKILLS

- Organization
- Knowledge of the English language
- Negotiation skills

NECESSARY SKILLS

- Computer literacy
- Financial knowledge
- Ability to communicate in writing

SUCCESS TIPS

- Cultivate an eye for detail
- Have knowledge of finances
- Have good networking skills

9 TO 5: HOW YOU WILL SPEND YOUR DAY

Many people have ideas about their financial goals, but these are little more than flights of fancy. Other people with financial goals have no clue about how to achieve them. Business plan writers provide a valuable service by turning these flights of fancy into well-mapped, feasible plans of action.

Business plan writers begin by interviewing clients to determine exactly what their goals are. This may be the most difficult part of the process, as clients may not have clear concepts of time frames, amounts, and locations. Usually, this information must be pried out of them through making suggestions and a process of elimination.

Once business plan writers have a general idea of what their clients want to achieve financially, they must examine the clients' financial information and current market research. From these, writers determine the feasibility of clients' goals and make changes wherever necessary. A feasible plan will describe the schedule, resource development, and spending.

WHERE YOU WILL SPEND YOUR DAY

Some business plan writers may be able to afford office space, but the vast majority operate from their own homes. Writers may determine their own hours, but success may depend greatly upon their flexibility and being available to clients on demand.

CAREER FORECAST

Although many people are searching for financial restructuring, the availability of self-help manuals and software might mean the demise of this career.

MONETARY REWARDS

Salaries can range from $20,000 to $100,000, due entirely to location and clientele affluence. Depending upon the amount of research and analysis necessary, fees may range from $2,000 to $5,000 per plan. Business plan writers must provide their own benefits.

UP THE LADDER

Advancement consists of increased clientele and an income large enough to begin a consulting firm. Success depends upon marketing and well-implemented business plans.

RELATED JOBS

- Employment counselor
- Management analyst
- Resume writer

GATHERING MORE FACTS

American Woman's Economic Development Corporation
216 East 45th Street, 10th Floor
New York, NY 10017
Internet: www.awed.org

Entrepreneurship Education at St. Louis University
Business Plan Advice
Internet: http://eweb.slu.edu/bpsites.htm

Small Business Administration
409 3rd Street, SW
Washington, DC 20416

Metro: Federal Center SW
Phone: (800) U-ASK-SBA
Internet: http://www.sba.gov/starting/

31. *Personnel Recruiter*

DEFINITION

Personnel recruiters search for and evaluate qualified candidates for specific job vacancies.

TRANSFERABLE TEACHING SKILLS

- Developing
- Verbalizing
- Discovering

NECESSARY SKILLS

- Good communication
- People skills
- Investigative ability

SUCCESS TIPS

- Be patient
- Be a good judge of people
- Be a good listener

9 TO 5: HOW YOU WILL SPEND YOUR DAY

Personnel recruiters regularly travel to colleges and universities in search of the most promising, best qualified students for potential employment. They review resumes sent to companies by job seekers. Personnel recruiters evaluate potential employees based on their education, technical skills, work history, managerial skills, salary requirements, and personalities. They give promotional presentations to inform qualified candidates of job opportunities and company benefits. They also check references, conduct follow-up interviews, evaluate the results, and maintain files on previously interviewed applicants.

One important aspect of a personnel recruiter's job is to understand and adhere to the company's policies on various types of discrimination. Recruiters should be aware of their company's needs, benefits, advancement policies, programs, and managerial structure.

Some personnel recruiters are employed by large corporations, others by private employment agencies that aid companies in finding qualified employees.

WHERE YOU WILL SPEND YOUR DAY

Personnel recruiters may travel a lot, usually to college campuses. Most have an office in a pleasant comfortable environment. Some work from their home. Because they travel so much, recruiters often must stay overnight out of town.

CAREER FORECAST

Much competition is predicted for job opportunities as a personnel recruiter. An abundance of highly qualified graduates will be applying for a limited number of openings.

MONETARY REWARDS

Personnel recruiters can expect to earn between $37,700 and $75,100 per year, depending on the size of the company or agency they work with. Benefits vary from company to company, but usually include medical insurance, vacations, and pension plans.

UP THE LADDER

Personnel recruiters typically have opportunities to advance to managerial positions within their company or agency. They may seek employment with larger companies that offer higher compensation.

RELATED JOBS

- Public relations specialist
- Counselor
- Social worker

GATHERING MORE FACTS

American Society for Training and Development
1640 King Street
P.O. Box 1443
Alexandria, VA 22313
Internet: www.astd.org

Recruiters OnLine Network, Inc.
3325 Landershire Lane, Suite 1001
Plano, TX 75023-6218
Phone: (800) 364-8425

Society for Human Resource Management
1800 Duke Street
Alexandria, Virginia 22314 USA
Phone: (703) 548-3440
Internet: www.shrm.org

32. *Employment Counselor*

DEFINITION

Employment counselors assist individuals and groups of individuals in making wise career decisions.

TRANSFERABLE TEACHING SKILLS

- Active listening
- Questioning
- Solving problems

Necessary Skills

- Good communication
- Interpersonal skills
- Knowledge of current employment trends

Success Tips

- Be able to read between the lines
- Work well with people
- Be a problem solver

9 to 5: How You Will Spend Your Day

Many people know that employment opportunities are excellent in this nation, but they often have no idea how to capitalize on them. Employment counselors provide the guidance necessary to get individuals onto the right track. Employment counselors ensure that clients are directed toward careers that they will be satisfied with, that they are capable of, and that will support them financially.

Counselors begin their work long before meeting their clients. Employment counselors collect information about current employment trends and requirements. Requirements often include specific college degrees and minimum experience levels.

Once counselors meet with clients, they must determine the clients' qualifications through information gathering and testing. Counselors collect information about clients' education, previous employment, skills, and interests, sometimes by administering aptitude and personality tests.

From the information gathered, the employment counselor determines potential careers and discusses these options with clients. The clients then determine which career to follow. Sometimes, employment counselors help clients with job placement.

Where You Will Spend Your Day

Employment counselors work in pleasant, quiet offices that emphasize the privacy of the counselor–client relationship.

> ## From Classroom to . . .
>
> "Before becoming an employment counselor, I was a high school guidance counselor. I helped students determine their interests and skills in order to develop goals for their college education. The skills I used with high school students were easily transferred to my current career. I really enjoy hearing from past clients who are very satisfied with their jobs."
>
> —JOHN GARCIA, *employment counselor*

Counselors usually work forty hours per week, although some of these may be evening hours to accommodate clients' current work schedules.

CAREER FORECAST

Employment opportunities in this field should grow quickly, as employers and employees alike realize the importance of satisfied workers.

MONETARY REWARDS

Salaries typically range from $24,000 to $40,000 a year, although some private counselors make much more. Benefits typically include vacations, health insurance, and pension plans.

UP THE LADDER

Advancement is generally into managerial or supervisory positions in government or private institutions, while self-employed counselors simply increase their clientele.

RELATED JOBS

- College and student personnel worker
- Occupational therapist
- Social worker

GATHERING MORE FACTS

American Counseling Association
5999 Stevenson Avenue
Alexandria, Virginia 22304-3300
Phone: (800) 347-6647
Internet: www.counseling.org

National Association of Personnel Services
3133 Mt. Vernon Avenue
Alexandria, VA 22305
Phone: (703) 684-0180

National Career Development Association
c/o Creative Management Alliance
10820 East 45th Street, Suite 210
Tulsa, OK 74146
Phone: (918) 663-7060
Internet: www.ncda.org

33. *Management Analyst/Consultant*

DEFINITION

Management analysts and consultants analyze and offer solutions to managerial problems.

TRANSFERABLE TEACHING SKILLS

- Leadership skills
- Ability to recommend ideas
- Interpreting data accurately

NECESSARY SKILLS

- Analytical thinking
- Good communication
- Creativity

Success Tips

- Clearly see the whole picture
- Make decisions quickly
- Determine long-term outcomes

9 TO 5: How You Will Spend Your Day

The responsibilities of management analysts and consultants vary, depending on the client and the project. Companies may employ a team of consultants, with each being responsible for a certain area, or they may need only one consultant to do the job. In both cases, the job has two phases. First, consultants gather, review, and analyze data. Second, they make suggestions to management on how to solve the discovered difficulties. They may even assist with implementation of the suggested proposals.

Once a contract is signed for a project, consultants or management analysts work to define the problem. This may involve analyzing employment records' annual revenues, as well as interviewing employees and managers. At the same time, the type of organization, its relationship with other businesses in the industry, and its organizational structure are also taken into account. After deciding on a course of action, consultants submit in writing their findings and recommendations to the client. They may also be required to give oral presentations of their findings.

Where You Will Spend Your Day

Management analysts and consultants split their work hours between their clients' sites and their offices. They generally work 40-hour weeks, but often log in uncompensated overtime hours in an attempt to meet project deadlines. Travel is frequent, because analysts and consultants spend a lot of time with clients.

Career Forecast

Employment opportunities are expected to increase through the next few years. This is due in part to industry's and government's increased reliance on independent sources to maximize the efficiency of their organizations. Federal, state, and local organizations are expected to increase their employment of management analysts and consultants.

MONETARY REWARDS

Salaries for management analysts and consultants vary widely. Earnings for analysts, which may include profit sharing and bonuses, average $39,000 annually. Entry-level consultants earn about $50,000 per year; management consultants, $70,000; senior consultants, $97,000; junior partners, $150,000; and senior partners, $266,000 per year. Benefits may include profit sharing and bonuses, vacations and sick leave, health and life insurance, and a retirement plan.

UP THE LADDER

With experience, analysts and consultants will gain more responsibility for projects and be able to establish their own hours. Those who demonstrate superior management skills could become partners in a firm. Those with entrepreneurial intentions may eventually be able to start their own firms.

RELATED JOBS

- Computer research analyst
- Financial analyst
- Operations

GATHERING MORE FACTS

Association of Career Management Consulting Firms
International
204 E Street, NE
Washington, DC 20002
Phone: (202) 547-6344
Internet: www.aocfi.org

Institute of Management Consultants
2025 M Street, NW, Suite 800
Washington, DC 20036-3309
Phone: (800) 221-2557
Internet: http://imcusa.org

International Council of Management Consulting
    Institutes
858 Longview Road
Burlingame, California 94010-6974
Phone: (650) 342-2250
Internet: www.icmci.org

34. *Customer Service Representative*

DEFINITION

Customer service representatives handle customer inquiries, gather customer information, and resolve customer problems, either in person or over the telephone.

TRANSFERABLE TEACHING SKILLS

- Fluency in the English language
- Good interpersonal skills
- Problem solving ability

NECESSARY SKILLS

- Keyboarding
- Patience
- Computer-use knowledge

SUCCESS TIPS

- A second language is helpful
- Cultivate a pleasant personality
- Maintain a professional appearance

9 TO 5: HOW YOU WILL SPEND YOUR DAY

Customer service representatives, often referred to as information clerks, are employed in nearly every industry. The duties of customer service representatives (CSRs) vary with the company in which they work. Some CSRs meet with the public and handle their duties in person. Other CSRs handle all duties over the telephone.

Employment for CSRs is concentrated in transportation, financial institutions, health service organizations, hotels and motels, and firms providing services for real estate and business.

Hotel, motel, and resort representatives have a variety of customer service duties. They register guests, assign rooms, and check out guests after their stay. Most of the information they handle is on computers. They often must answer questions about the local community, such as restaurant recommendations, entertainment opportunities, or directions to a specific address. They must also handle customer complaints.

Interviewing and new accounts customer service representatives gather information from customers of banks, medical offices, or companies conducting surveys or research.

In banks, CSRs help customers open new accounts, answer inquiries about services, and refer customers to sales personnel. Although most CSRs work directly with customers in local offices, more financial institutions are developing call centers that provide twenty-four-hour-a-day service to customers.

In medical facilities, CSRs gather information from patients being admitted to a hospital or seeking treatment in a doctor's office. CSRs record a patient's personal and medical information into a computer to create or update a patient's file. Sometimes the CSR must verify a patient's insurance carrier or set up payment plans.

Receptionists are another type of customer service representative. They play a vital role in the success of a business. Customers of many businesses meet the receptionist first. Receptionists set the tone for the business. They direct calls and inquiries to individuals who can provide specific answers or services for the customer. They often must operate multiline telephones, use a computer system, and operate a fax machine. In addition, they may assist other employees by setting up appointments, taking messages, transmitting and receiving faxes, and even helping to make travel plans.

The travel industry employs CSRs to sell tickets, confirm reservations, check luggage, and provide travel information to tourists. Reservation clerks often work for hotels or airlines and help customers plan trips and make reservations. They quote prices for rooms or fares. Transportation ticket agents work in airports as well as train and bus stations. They sell tickets, assign seats to passengers, and check travelers' bags. They may also help passengers board or disembark, help the elderly or disabled, and check boarding passes. Travel clerks work for organizations such as auto clubs. They help customers plan trips, offer travel suggestions, create travel itineraries, help with hotel and restaurant reservations, and secure car rentals.

Where You Will Spend Your Day

Most customer service representatives work in offices or centralized call centers that are clean, well lit, and quiet. Many CSRs work a 40-hour week, although some CSR jobs may require evening, late night, weekend, and holiday shifts. Some call centers may need a staff twenty-four hours a day. In general, CSRs with less seniority will be expected to work the less desirable shifts.

Career Forecast

Because of high turnover in the customer service field, many job opportunities will arise in the near future. Steady growth in the motel and hotel industry and the health service industry will produce numerous job openings. Job opportunities in the transportation industry will be more limited, as consumers increasingly use technology such as Internet travel services.

MONETARY REWARDS

Earnings for customer service representatives vary considerably, depending on the location, size, and type of business. Representatives who work evenings, nights, weekends, or holidays frequently receive shift differential pay. The average annual salary ranges from $15,000 up to $39,500. Benefits usually include health and life insurance, pension plans, vacation and sick leave, and, occasionally, educational assistance. CSRs in the travel industry may receive reduced or free travel rates for themselves or family members.

UP THE LADDER

Opportunities for promotion are usually in the form of transfers to positions with more responsibility or supervisory positions. Additional training or education improves an individual's opportunities for advancement.

RELATED JOBS

- Telephone operator
- Travel agent
- Records processing clerk

GATHERING MORE FACTS

Air Transport Association of America
1301 Pennsylvania Avenue, NW, Suite 1100
Washington, DC 20004-1707
Phone: (202) 626-4000
Internet: www.airlines.org

Communication Workers of America
Research Department
501 Third Street NW
Washington, DC 20001
Phone: (202) 434-1100
Internet: www.cwa-union.org

The Educational Institute of the American Hotel and
   Lodging Association
800 North Magnolia Avenue, Suite 1800
Orlando, FL 32803
Phone: (800) 752-4567
Internet: http://www.ei-ahma.org

35. *Translator*

DEFINITION

Translators translate written documents from one language to
another.

TRANSFERABLE TEACHING SKILLS

- Patience
- Interpreting skills
- Translating skills

NECESSARY SKILLS

- Good communication
- Keyboarding skills
- Reliability

SUCCESS TIPS

- Be trustworthy
- Be able to think in both languages
- Be self-motivated

9 TO 5: HOW YOU WILL SPEND YOUR DAY

In the global village that our world is quickly becoming, swift
translation between native languages is essential to maintain
the communications link forged by entertainment and technol-

ogy. Until language translation software improves, translators will be necessary mediators between cultures.

Translators used to attend international meetings to translate spoken words to those who could not understand. Although this still happens, a growing lucrative business is the translation of written words, from romance novels to confidential legal documents. Most of this work is received through the Internet and then translated by translators on their own computers, usually at home. The translated work is shipped back though the Internet when complete.

Translating can be long and tedious work, but a large market exists for it. A little marketing through translation associations and yellow page advertisements should provide a wealth of business for translators, particularly if they have expertise in any specialized terminology—medical, legal, financial, and so on. Eastern language translators are in the highest demand.

WHERE YOU WILL SPEND YOUR DAY

Translators work wherever they desire to work, assuming they can afford the space. Typically, they operate from within the comfort of their own homes. They set their own work hours, but this freedom may be restricted by employer deadlines.

CAREER FORECAST

The increased globalization of our economy ensures rapid growth in this field.

MONETARY REWARDS

Fees average from 5 to 50 cents per word, although these fees may fluctuate according to language complexity, special terminology, and length. More common languages, such as Spanish, pay less than rare languages, such as Latvian. Translators must arrange their own benefits.

Up the Ladder

Advancement comes through reliable translations and specialization in uncommon terminology. Usually, this advancement means more difficult assignments at higher fees.

Related Jobs

- Bilingual consultant
- Linguist
- Sign language interpreter

Gathering More Facts

American Translators Association
225 Reinekers Lane, Suite 590
Alexandria, VA 22314
Telephone: (703) 683-6100
Internet: www.atanet.org

National Association of Judiciary Interpreters and
    Translators (NAJIT)
551 Fifth Avenue, Suite 3025
New York, NY 10176
Phone: (212) 692-9581
Internet: www.najit.org

From Classroom to . . .

"When I taught high school Spanish, I had to pay attention to language patterns, grammar, and the idiomatic meaning of the language. I had to listen carefully to my students' speaking and speak clearly to them in Spanish and English. I believe my success or any translator's successful career is based on these important qualities. My part-time interpreting for the local courts quickly turned into a full-time freelance interpreting career."

—Amanda Wilson, *freelance translator*

Translators and Interpreters Guild
2007 North 15th Street, Suite 4
Arlington, VA 22201-2621
Phone: (800) 992-0367
Internet: www.ttig.org

36. *Fundraiser*

DEFINITION

Professional fundraisers solicit donations and set up fund drives from individuals and corporations for colleges, charities, hospitals, and other nonprofit organizations.

TRANSFERABLE TEACHING SKILLS

- Ascertaining
- Motivating
- Explaining

NECESSARY SKILLS

- Good communication
- Managerial skills
- Interpersonal skills

SUCCESS TIPS

- Have a working knowledge of finance and tax laws
- Manifest drive and ambition
- Be honest

9 TO 5: HOW YOU WILL SPEND YOUR DAY

The first task for fundraisers is to decide how much money the client needs. This figure is added to the amount estimated for the cost of the fundraising campaign. Next, the campaign is planned to determine its length, the type of publishing necessary to promote the event, and what slogans will be used during the campaign. They also decide who will solicit the funds and how they will do it. They assess the progress of the campaign, analyze its strong and weak points, and determine corrections to make to ensure success in future campaigns.

Fundraisers are employed either full time or as consultants. Fundraisers working as consultants for companies occupy office space on a temporary basis, which allows them an opportunity to meet with management when necessary.

WHERE YOU WILL SPEND YOUR DAY

Fundraisers work irregular hours, which may include nights and weekends. If working on national campaigns, they may travel frequently. They may have office space or may work from their home, depending on the size of their campaign and who their employer is.

CAREER FORECAST

The employment outlook for professional fundraisers is very good. Because this field is relatively new and small, experienced fundraisers are in great demand.

MONETARY REWARDS

Fundraisers' salaries vary, depending on the employer and location of the industry. Salaries average about $44,000 a year. More experienced fundraisers may earn more than $90,000. Benefits could include health insurance, paid holidays and vacations, and pension plans.

UP THE LADDER

Professional fundraisers, with experience, can eventually become directors of fundraising programs. Some begin their own firms or become directors of other consulting firms. Most fundraisers eventually seek advancement to more attractive

> ## From Classroom to . . .
>
> "I have always found a great joy and fulfillment in helping young people learn. As a teacher, I was able to get kids excited about learning and to want to learn even more," says James Ward, a *director of development and alumni relations* for a private Illinois university. "I can continue to cultivate that learning by raising money so they can attend college. Because I know I have a great impact on students' lives, I'm motivated to excel at my job."

positions by assuming responsibility for bigger campaigns with bigger companies.

RELATED JOBS

- Campaign worker
- Lobbyist
- Media specialist

GATHERING MORE FACTS

American Association of Fundraising Counsel
10293 North Meridian Street, Suite 175
Indianapolis, IN 46290
Phone: (800) 462-2372
Internet: www.aafrc.org

National Committee on Planned Giving
233 McCrea Street, Suite 400
Indianapolis, Indiana 46225
Phone: (317) 269-6274
Internet: www.ncpg.org

National Society of Fund-Raising Executives
1101 King Street, Suite 700

Alexandria, VA 22314-2967
Phone: (703) 684-0410
Internet: www.nsfre.org

37. Convention Specialist

DEFINITION

Convention specialists direct and supervise convention activities for companies and organizations.

TRANSFERABLE TEACHING SKILLS

- Monitoring
- Verbalizing
- Scheduling

NECESSARY SKILLS

- Communication skills
- Problem-solving ability
- Precision (eye for detail)

SUCCESS TIPS

- Be able to solve problems quickly
- Coordinate effectively
- When troubleshooting, think "outside the box"

9 TO 5: HOW YOU WILL SPEND YOUR DAY

With the general increase of wealth and spare time in this nation, many organizations and companies are able to devote a portion of their efforts to conducting a variety of conventions, business-related meetings ranging from one-day training seminars to week-long research and development conventions. However, companies and organizations rarely want to spend the time and money required to attend to every detail of a convention. Often, these institutions find it cheaper to hire professional convention specialists, either as full-time staff for institutions that have numerous conventions or as a contracted consultant and organizer.

Sometimes an institution's executives may choose a convention site in advance, but other times convention specialists must find a site and have it approved by their employers and the site's management personnel. Once a site is determined, the convention specialist spends long hours developing a convention schedule, which includes meetings, classes, recreational activities, and social functions.

The approval of a complete convention schedule moves the specialist on to the preparation of the site, where the site's facilities are developed as necessary for the activities of the convention. Then, during the actual convention, the specialist must be present to ensure that all runs smoothly.

WHERE YOU WILL SPEND YOUR DAY

Convention specialists operate from comfortable offices, but are usually found in meetings with employers or on site, developing future conventions. Work hours are often long and irregular, requiring evening and weekend work at times. Travel may be necessary to visit distant convention sites.

CAREER FORECAST

The increase in conventions and the benefits to local economics where conventions are held have made conditions favorable to the continued growth of this field.

MONETARY REWARDS

Convention specialists earn salaries ranging from $38,000 to $55,000 a year, although these figures vary according to the size and location of the conventions they plan. Benefits include possible travel, vacations, medical insurance, and pension plans.

Up the Ladder

Convention specialists may advance to executive positions in the employing organizations, or freelancers may develop their own consulting firms. Success depends upon the number and size of planned conventions.

Related Jobs

* Event planner
* Fundraiser
* Interior designer

Gathering More Facts

Association for Convention Marketing Executives
2965 Flowers Road South, Suite 105
Atlanta, GA 30341
Phone: (770) 454-6111
Internet: www.acmenet.org

International Association of Convention and Visitor
    Bureaus
2000 L Street, NW, Suite 702

From Classroom to . . .

"When I was a teacher, I was the coordinator for the parent/teacher annual school carnival. The organizational and planning skills I learned from that event were the base for the skills needed as a convention planning consultant. I find my job very fulfilling and satisfying because I enjoy taking an event from its initial concept; adding in the imagination, creativity, and enthusiasm of my staff; and presenting a convention, conference, or seminar that people enjoy."

—Julie London, *convention specialist*

Washington, DC 20036-4990
Phone: (202) 296-7888
Internet: www.iacvb.org

Professional Convention Management Association
2301 South Lake Shore Drive, Suite 1001
Chicago, IL 60616-1419
Phone: (312) 423-7262
Internet: www.pcma.org

Computers 'R' Us

Career opportunities in the computer and Internet industries are growing at a phenomenal rate. Some teachers gain experience using computers in their classrooms. Others even receive additional training in the computer field and become the school "techies." Practical experience with computers is a good base to build on if you're considering a career change into the computer field.

A career in computers can provide good money, job security, career advancement, job mobility, and excellent benefits. Although competition for these jobs can be high in some geographical locations, opportunities exist all over the country. New jobs will be created in multimedia, with online services, and through the Internet. If you want to get your career onto the fast track, check out this chapter, where we explore careers in the computer field.

38. Computer Programmer

DEFINITION

Computer programmers write instructions in languages or codes that computers understand and that tell computers how to process data.

Transferable Teaching Skills

* Diligence
* Persistence
* Reasoning ability

Necessary Skills

* Computer literacy
* Logical/mathematical skills
* Problem solving ability

Success Tips

* Be able to sit for long periods of time
* Be patient
* Be persistent

9 to 5: How You Will Spend Your Day

Two categories of computer programmers exist: systems programmers and applications programmers. Systems programmers write the instructions that coordinate the activities of the processors, memory boards, input devices, and output devices of a computer. Applications programmers write instructions to complete tasks through the use of computerized technology. The instructions written by applications programmers operate within the confines of those instructions programmed by systems programmers. Essentially, systems programmers create the computerized environment, while applications programmers create smaller programs that utilize their environment to fulfill very specific, data processing tasks.

The specifications for programs are usually given to computer programmers by systems analysts, who determine the needs of a business. Occasionally, a programmer, called a programmer-analyst, will perform both tasks. However the request is relayed to programmers, they must then analyze the nature and length of the necessary program to determine a suitable language and control structure. Once these parameters are determined, programmers must efficiently create the instructions, test the program, and then correct any programming errors. When the program is operational, the programmer must create an instruction sheet or manual on the use of the program.

WHERE YOU WILL SPEND YOUR DAY

Programmers usually work in pleasant, dust-free offices. Travel is occasionally necessary for on-site programming. Work hours are usually 35 to 40 per week, but night and weekend work may be necessary to meet deadlines or observe trial runs of a program.

CAREER FORECAST

The steady demand for more efficient, smaller, faster, and more user-friendly programs ensures that the computer programming field will grow for a long time.

MONETARY REWARDS

Salaries range from $20,000 to more than $65,000 per year, depending upon location and experience. Programmers for major software and hardware companies are the highest-paid programmers. Benefits typically include vacations, group insurance, and pension plans.

UP THE LADDER

Programming experience provides a variety of advancement options. Some programmers move to administrative positions, while others move into systems analysis departments. Still others enjoy and move into research and development. The greatest difficulty is in determining where to advance.

From Classroom to . . .

Many skills that Les White used as a high school computer teacher help him in his new job as a *computer programmer.* He has now been programming for more than ten years. In some ways his new job is similar to teaching:

- The challenge: Everything constantly changes
- The continual learning process
- The freedom to be creative

New things he enjoys are:

- Seeing that programs I created work
- The pay
- Not having to meet daily quotas

RELATED JOBS

- Computer engineer
- Operations research analyst
- Statistician

GATHERING MORE FACTS

American Society for Information Science
1320 Fenwick Lane, Suite 510
Silver Spring, MD 20910
Phone: (301) 495-0900
Internet: www.asis.org

Association for Computing Machinery
One Astor Plaza
1515 Broadway
New York, NY 10036
Phone: (212) 869-7440
Internet: www.acm.org

Association of Information Technology Professionals
315 South Northwest Highway, Suite 200
Park Ridge, IL 60068-4278
Phone: (800) 224-9371
Internet: www.aitp.org

39. *Webmaster*

DEFINITION

A webmaster designs and organizes World Wide Web sites for corporations and other large institutions.

TRANSFERABLE TEACHING SKILLS

- Computer knowledge
- Investigative talent
- Ability to develop ideas

NECESSARY SKILLS

- Creativity
- Writing ability
- Marketing skills

SUCCESS TIPS

- Have a love of technology
- Be a problem solver
- Enjoy working independently

9 TO 5: HOW YOU WILL SPEND YOUR DAY

In order to remain competitive in attracting consumer attention, institutions must ensure that their Web sites remain on the cutting edge of marketing techniques and consumer–computer interactivity. Without the direction of a specialist, viewers would quickly lose interest in Web sites if they kept observing the same data in the same format. Webmasters ensure that Web sites remain dynamically competitive.

Webmasters first must secure space on the World Wide Web for the sites they develop. They do this by contracting with an Internet service provider to serve as a storage facility for the site and all of its accompanying information. Webmasters also establish URLs (Uniform Resource Locators), which serve as addresses for their sites, through registration with Inter NIC.

Usually, webmasters are given the textual content of the Web sites to be created, although they may have to provide content as well, using general guidelines. The webmaster takes the text and graphics and arranges this information on a series of pages. Webmasters use HTML (Hyper Text Markup Language) to format these pages so that they will appear on the computer as designed. The resulting Web pages must be visually pleasing, interactive whenever necessary, and easily navigated. These sites must also be maintained and updated.

WHERE YOU WILL SPEND YOUR DAY

Webmasters primarily work alone at computers in pleasant, dust-free offices. They must sometimes interact with various other departments to develop new sites and modify existing sites. Larger organizations may have full teams of webmasters. Work hours are usually forty per week, although overtime may occasionally be necessary to meet company deadlines.

CAREER FORECAST

The exponential evolution and growth of the Internet in content and usage ensure that this field will grow at a rapid pace.

MONETARY REWARDS

Salaries range from less than $25,000 to more than $110,000 per year, depending upon location, one's experience, and the

From Classroom to . . .

Pauline Walker finds being a *webmaster* a great career move after teaching high school business. "I work from my home office so I can set my own work schedule. Occasionally, I have to meet face-to-face with clients, but most work can be done from my office. I recently began using online conferencing, which allows me to have real-time conferences with clients and their staff. I could handle nearly every aspect of my business from my office, but I like going to visit my clients on site. This allows me to get a better idea of their business, which helps me create and maintain a more effective Web site for them."

size of the employer. Benefits may include vacations, health insurance, pension plans, and even bonuses or stock options.

UP THE LADDER

Advancement in large organizations consists of promotion to supervisory positions over teams of webmasters. Others advance by starting their own businesses, moving to more profitable institutions, or moving to new fields.

RELATED JOBS

- Computer trainer
- Internet content developer
- Web site creator

GATHERING MORE FACTS

International Webmaster Association
119 East Union Street, Suite E
Pasadena, CA 91101

Phone: (626) 449-3709
Internet: www.iwanet.org

Webmasters Guild
Internet: www.webmasters.org

World Organization of Webmasters
9580 Oak Avenue Parkway, Suite 7-177
Folsom, CA 95630
Phone: (916) 608-1597
Internet: www.joinwow.org

40. *Computer Trainer/Tutor*

DEFINITION

Computer trainers teach people how to more effectively utilize their computers in the workplace or school.

TRANSFERABLE TEACHING SKILLS

- Motivating
- Overseeing
- Inspiring

NECESSARY SKILLS

- Patience
- Good communication
- Interpersonal skills

SUCCESS TIPS

- Have a love of computers
- Have good people skills
- Be able to train effectively

9 to 5: How You Will Spend Your Day

The explosion of the computer industry in the early 1980s caught many people with their defenses down, and some are unable to recover from their shock at computers' capabilities. These people often don't have the time, energy, or money to invest to catch up with our technological society. Some of the most advanced computer users have trouble maintaining up-to-date computer literacy. Computer trainers take advantage of individual desires and corporate needs for computer-literate employees, to form a lucrative career field.

Computer trainers must have certification for the courses they teach. Certification requires meeting the standards of the International Board of Standards for Training, Performance, and Instruction. Trainers must analyze, understand, and prepare course materials and the teaching site. They must demonstrate effective communication, presentation, and questioning skills. Trainers must be able to interact with learners in the following ways: respond to needs for clarification, provide positive reinforcement, provide motivational incentives, and evaluate performances. Most trainers utilize a variety of instructional tools, such as CD-ROMs, multimedia presentations, the Internet, and intranets.

Where You Will Spend Your Day

Computer trainers usually work in comfortable offices, but a large part of their time is spent in classrooms and training facilities. Work hours are usually forty per week, but traveling to training sites may increase these hours.

Career Forecast

The increased use of computers ensures that computer literacy will be a major issue in the future, thus guaranteeing fast growth in the computer training field.

Monetary Rewards

The average salary is about $40,000 per year, although managerial positions promise as much as $60,000 per year. Benefits include medical and dental insurance, vacations, and yearly bonuses ranging from $1,600 to $5,200.

Up the Ladder

Graduate and postgraduate education practically guarantees advancement in large companies. Advancement is into supervisory positions, such as training specialists, senior training specialists, and training managers.

Related Jobs

- Database design analyst
- Hardware engineer
- Technical support specialist

Gathering More Facts

Association for Development, Advancement and
     Productivity through Technology Training
c/o Helene Weitzenkorn
34 Slocum Road
Jamaica Plain, MA 02130
Phone: (617) 522-5918
Internet: www.adapttrain.org

International Association of Information Technology
     Trainers
9810 Patuxent Woods Drive
Columbia, MD 21046-1561
Phone: (410) 290-7000
Internet: www.itrain.org

Society for Technical Communication
901 North Stuart Street, Suite 904

From Classroom to . . .

Computers are second nature to Darrin Zink because he has used them since high school in the early 1980s. "I learned BASIC programming from my high school computer teacher. As computers evolved, I learned how to use the new features. In 1987, I graduated from college with a secondary math teaching degree and started teaching several computer classes to the students. Much of the knowledge I have of computer use and programming is self-taught. When people started asking me to help them set up their computers and teach them how to use them, I realized I could start a *computer training and tutoring business.* I worked with individuals and offered classes to small groups. Four years ago, I decided to leave the classroom and pursue the training and tutoring business full time. I still offer training for individuals, but much of my business is with groups, including corporate training sessions. It's rewarding to be able to make a living at something I enjoy so much."

Arlington, Virginia 22203-1822
Phone: (703) 522-4114
Internet: www.stc.org

41. *Internet Content Developer*

DEFINITION

Internet content developers, or Web designers/developers, create and modify Internet sites.

TRANSFERABLE TEACHING SKILLS

* Creativity
* Computer skills
* Ability to meet deadlines

NECESSARY SKILLS

- Creativity
- Ability to work quickly
- Flexibility

SUCCESS TIPS

- Be a good listener
- Have a love of computers
- Be able to work independently

9 TO 5: HOW YOU WILL SPEND YOUR DAY

The explosion of the Internet came about because of the vast communication possibilities hidden in its ones and zeros. Once people realized the extent of these possibilities, traffic on the Web increased innumerable times over. However, all of this traffic requires people to program the technology necessary to continue it. One of these individuals is the Internet content developer, who creates Web sites.

Internet content developers begin their work by first determining the attributes of the desired Web sites. Each site has overall goals, a layout, and performance limitations attributed to it, although the site's developer might not choose these. When these parameters are chosen, developers design the Web sites accordingly. Then, they write the program code needed to run the Web sites.

A site concept is translated into a layout that must be turned into a series of pages. Each page, once designed, is then coded. Developers may use software packages that perform coding operations for them; but because these packages use templates, the finished product lacks originality, which is necessary to attract attention. The developer serves as the intermediary between the company and the customer.

Where You Will Spend Your Day

Internet content developers spend most of their time alone at a computer in pleasant, dust-free offices. Contact with others is limited to conversations on the Internet and with supervisors. Individual developers may determine their work hours, as long as company deadlines are met.

Career Forecast

The rapid evolution and growth of the Internet ensures that opportunities as an Internet developer will grow quickly.

Monetary Rewards

Salaries range from $30,000 to $74,000 yearly, with an average of $50,000 per year for experienced developers. Salaries depend upon the location, one's experience, and the size of the employer. Benefits typically include vacations, health, dental, and life insurance as well as bonuses.

Up the Ladder

Advancement consists of moving to a larger company or becoming a webmaster. Webmasters are essentially supervisory positions over Internet content developers.

Related Jobs

- Webmaster
- Web site creator
- Internet security specialist

Gathering More Facts

Association for Computing Machinery
One Astor Plaza
1515 Broadway

New York, NY 10036-5701
Phone: (212) 869-7440
Internet: www.acm.org/

Association of Internet Professionals
2629 Main Street #136
Santa Monica, CA 90405
Phone: (609) 737-6842
Internet: www.association.org

World Wide Web Consortium
Internet: www.w3c.org

42. *Internet Security Specialist*

DEFINITION

Internet security specialists protect a company's network, accessible through the Internet, from outside intrusions.

TRANSFERABLE TEACHING SKILLS

- Flexibility
- Ability to solve problems
- Eye for detail

NECESSARY SKILLS

- Good communication
- Organization
- Creativity

SUCCESS TIPS

- Discover the problem
- Monitor the system thoroughly
- Investigate possible solutions

9 to 5: How You Will Spend Your Day

With the introduction of every new technology, there is someone who seeks to abuse, harm, or destroy that technology. Internet communications are no exception to this rule. Because of the ever-present danger of hackers, or people who attempt to break into computer systems through the use of the Internet, security must be created to either prevent their intrusions or warn of their attempts. Internet security specialists are responsible for these security measures.

The primary duty of the Internet security specialist is the construction of firewalls for employers. Firewalls are systems that restrict or limit access to a computer or network through the Internet. Specialists monitor the flow of information through these firewalls, usually through logs and alerts. Strange activity requires investigation, the creation of an improved firewall, or both.

Secondary duties of an Internet security specialist include security administration and security engineering, both of which deal with the internal security of a network. Security administrative duties typically involve the creation, implementation, and distribution of security policies for Internet usage. Security engineering duties involve monitoring internal computer traffic to ensure that security policies are adhered to.

Where You Will Spend Your Day

Internet security specialists spend most of their time alone at computers in pleasant, dust-free offices. Contact with others is limited to conversations on the Internet and with employers. Work hours are usually 40 to 50 per week, although security breaches may require overtime work to fix them as soon as possible.

Career Forecast

The increased connection of private company networks to the Internet ensures that this field will grow, as owners seek to protect their information. Demand for specialists currently exceeds the supply.

Monetary Rewards

Salaries range from $25,000 to $120,000 per year, although most specialists earn from $50,000 to $75,000 per year. Benefits include vacations, health and dental insurance, and bonuses.

Up the Ladder

Advancement comes through seniority within the same company or by moving to another, larger company. Some private consultants who become very good at security may become "sneakers," people who hack into security systems to find out which areas need to be improved.

Related Jobs

- Computer programmer
- Internet content developer
- Security consultant and technician

Gathering More Facts

Association of Information Technology Professionals
315 South Northwest Highway, Suite 200
Park Ridge, IL 60068-4278
Phone: (800) 224-9371
Internet: www.aitp.org

Association of Internet Professionals
2629 Main Street, #136
Santa Monica, CA 90405
Phone: (609) 737-6842
Internet: www.association.org

US Internet Industry Association
919 18th Street, 10th Floor

Washington, DC 20006
Phone: (202) 496-9007
Internet: www.usiia.org

43. *Computer Network Administrator*

DEFINITION

Computer network administrators design, install, and maintain the various network services and Internet systems of corporations and other institutions.

TRANSFERABLE TEACHING SKILLS

* Patience
* Ability to supervise
* Computer knowledge

NECESSARY SKILLS

* Organization skills
* Problem solving ability
* Good communication

SUCCESS TIPS

* Be able to organize and lead a group
* Cultivate time-management skills
* Integrate systems thoroughly, "covering all bases"

9 TO 5: HOW YOU WILL SPEND YOUR DAY

Originally, computer users simultaneously accessing the same information did so through a mainframe connected to several "dumb" terminals. Effectively, they all used one computer. The updating failings of this method, however, drove many corporations to local area networking and wide area networking (LAN and WAN) systems that update all client computers nearly instantaneously. These systems also allow several computers to make use of the same peripheral devices, such as printers and modems, without requiring individual devices at each computer. Networks consist of several computers that tap into the resources of one central computer, but each computer can operate separately from the others. Computer network administrators oversee the design, installation, and maintenance of these networks.

Computer network administrators are responsible for updating files and applications of the central computer, called a server. They must also ensure that peripheral devices shared by the computer recognize a priority list of which computer's demands to complete first. Administrators set up user access and security measures to protect confidential information stored on the server. Administrators monitor and record network traffic. They must field all problems that users may have with the network, particularly the communications aspect of the network.

WHERE YOU WILL SPEND YOUR DAY

Computer network administrators work at computers in pleasant, dust-free offices. Work hours range from 40 to 50 per week, although overtime is common among administrators who must install or repair networks.

CAREER FORECAST

The increased use of networks to handle corporate operations ensures that this field will grow quickly.

MONETARY REWARDS

Computer network administrators earn from $46,000 to $72,000 per year, with the average salary being about $55,000 per year. Benefits include vacations, health insurance, pension plans, and tuition reimbursement programs for those continuing their education.

From Classroom to ...

Dave Campbell started out teaching high school math, but his interest in computers led to a position as the school corporation's *network administrator.* "I took a class about network management after the school implemented a LAN. I guess you could say I was the school's 'techie.' As I worked with the network, my interest grew and I pursued a computer science degree and certification that would enable me to be a network administrator. As the school corporation's network administrator, I oversee the networks of nine elementary schools, three middle schools, and a large high school. I enjoy working with the teachers and knowing that I still have an impact on the learning of our students."

UP THE LADDER

Administrators may be promoted to network manager or network engineer positions. They may also cross over into other related fields, such as computer programming and systems analysis. Continuing education and experience are important for all advancement.

RELATED JOBS

- Internet security specialist
- Security consultant
- Webmaster

GATHERING MORE FACTS

Association for Computing Machinery
1515 Broadway
New York, NY 10036-5701
Phone: (212) 869-7440
Internet: www.acm.org

Institute for Certification of Computing Professionals
2350 East Devon Avenue, Suite 115
Des Plaines, IL 60018
Phone: (800) 843-8227
Internet: www.iccp.org

Network Professional Association
195 South C Street, Suite 250
Tustin, CA 92780
Phone: (714) 573-4780
Internet: www.npa.org

44. *Online Researcher*

DEFINITION

Online researchers, also called information brokers or independent information professionals, prepare reports and presentations from information they have compiled from online sources.

TRANSFERABLE TEACHING SKILLS

- Good research skills
- Linguistic intelligence
- Editing ability

NECESSARY SKILLS

- Good communication
- Ability to motivate people
- Organizational skills

SUCCESS TIPS

- Be creative in marketing
- Have a love of computers
- Be able to locate specific information

9 TO 5: HOW YOU WILL SPEND YOUR DAY

With the vast amount of information that is available through the Internet, it is nearly impossible for someone with limited time or energy to find all of the information that would be helpful, particularly in the research of obscure topics. Online researchers provide corporations and other institutions with the tedious service of tracking down all such information and compiling it into an intelligible format. Online researchers are essentially the librarians of the Internet.

Online researchers must have skills similar to those of private investigators and librarians. They must be able to sift through vast amounts of information. Such sifting requires expert knowledge on using most of the available online databases and search engines, such as Alta Vista, Infoseek, Dialog, Lexis/Nexis, Yahoo!, Library of Congress, and many others. Each database or search engine has particular request formats and keywords that are especially effective. An online researcher must be aware of these peculiarities to be successful.

After gathering information on a topic, the researcher must compile it and give it to the employer. Although some online researchers work full time within institutions, many more operate as independent researchers who must market their skills to be successful.

WHERE YOU WILL SPEND YOUR DAY

Independent researchers work at home, while corporate researchers work in pleasant, dust-free offices. Independent researchers work 50 to 60 hours a week, while corporate researchers usually work 40 to 50 hours a week. Travel may occasionally be necessary to meet with clients and to find information not attainable through the Internet.

CAREER FORECAST

Because of the expansion of the Internet, this career field should grow about as fast as the average career.

Monetary Rewards

Earnings range from $20,000 to $100,000 a year, with the average being equal to that of the full-time special librarian, $45,500 a year. Benefits for corporate researchers include health insurance, vacations, and bonuses. Independent researchers must provide their own benefits.

Up the Ladder

Advancement depends upon marketing, promotion, and building a client base. Some researchers begin through specialization, but advancement, in the form of bigger, higher-paying projects, comes through generalizing search capabilities.

Related Jobs

- Virtual office services
- Indexer
- Professional organizer

Gathering More Facts

Association of Independent Information Professionals
7044 South 13th Street
Oak Creek, WI 53154-1429
Phone: (414) 766-0421
Internet: www.aiip.org

Society of Computer Professionals
20 Acorn Road
Secaucus, NJ 07094
Phone: (201) 865-0827
Internet: www.comprof.com

US Internet Industry Association
919 18th Street, 10th Floor
Washington, DC 20006

Phone: (202) 496-9007
Internet: www.usiia.org

45. *Computer Support Service Owners*

DEFINITION

The owners of computer support services assist individuals and businesses with installations and maintenance of computer software and hardware.

TRANSFERABLE TEACHING SKILLS

- Developing
- Computer skills
- Patience

NECESSARY SKILLS

- Good communication
- Management skills
- Teaching ability

SUCCESS TIPS

- Explain things clearly
- Be able to diagnose problems
- Instruct people using laymen's terms

9 TO 5: HOW YOU WILL SPEND YOUR DAY

Computer support service owners, also called computer consultants, aid people with difficult hardware and software. Although modern computer equipment has been designed to be more user-friendly, it is often too complicated to be installed by typical users. Some equipment is still not user-friendly enough to be utilized without some training. Computer consultants provide these services, often through hardware and software manufacturers. Computer consultants begin their work by accepting calls from clients, both new and regular. Clients describe the problems to their consultants, who then determine whether each problem can be solved through telephone instruction. If this is not the case for a particular problem, consultants will supply themselves with the necessary equipment and make on-site visits to correct the problem. Problems can range from an incorrectly connected wire to faulty hardware to a virus.

Some computer consultants expand their businesses by offering other services. The growth of the Internet has led some consultants to offer Web site–related services, while others help create databases and programs.

WHERE YOU WILL SPEND YOUR DAY

Computer support service owners usually operate from home offices or rented commercial spaces, although most of their time is spent in on-site consultations. Both locations are typically pleasant, dust-free offices. Most owners work more than 40-hour weeks.

CAREER FORECAST

Our growing reliance on computers and the increase of computer complexity ensure that computer support service owners will be needed for a long time.

MONETARY REWARDS

Earnings range from $40,000 to more than $100,500 per year, with the average annual earnings being $60,000. Earnings depend upon location, range of services, and clientele base. As self-employed workers, consultants must provide their own benefits.

Up the Ladder

Advancement usually comes through expansion and the variety of services offered, such as training sessions, multimedia presentation preparation, and Web site design. Advancement through an increased client base may allow a consultant to employ a full-time staff.

Related Jobs

- Health regulatory inspector
- Internet security specialist
- Security consultant

Gathering More Facts

Association for Computing Machinery
1515 Broadway
New York, NY 10036-5701
Phone: (212) 869-7440
Internet: www.acm.org

Association of Computer Support Specialists
218 Huntington Road
Bridgeport, CT 06608
Phone: (203) 332-1524
Internet: www.acss.org

Independent Computer Consultants Association
11131 South Town Square, Suites F
St. Louis, MO 63123
Phone: (800) 774-4222
Internet: www.icca.org

46. *Web Site Editor*

DEFINITION

Web site editors organize and edit online magazines that focus on particular subjects or marketing groups.

TRANSFERABLE TEACHING SKILLS

- Eye for detail
- Knowledge of the English language
- Computer knowledge

NECESSARY SKILLS

- Creativity
- Marketing skills
- Writing ability

SUCCESS TIPS

- Be able to work independently
- Handle the pressure of deadlines
- Have knowledge of layout design

9 TO 5: HOW YOU WILL SPEND YOUR DAY

Along with the general growth of the Internet's content and usage, many people now direct their efforts toward providing specific information about their expertise. These people, Web site editors, have tapped into the vast communication power of the Internet to reach a wide audience with their "magazines." These online magazines, ranging from a few Web pages to the length of several directories in size, contain regularly updated information about a variety of topics. Usually, each magazine is dedicated to a particular topic, such as dog breeding or skiing, or to a particular audience, such as high school gothic teens.

Web site editors develop and maintain these magazines with information that is personally gleaned from experience or outside sources. The success of a magazine depends upon the marketing skills of the magazine's editor. The editor must be able to take advantage of online marketing techniques, such as content trade-off and links to similarly oriented sites. Another useful marketing scheme is to tap into the Internet community that has an interest in existing sites with similar topics and then to spread the news of the magazine. Word-of-mouth interest will increase the number of people who at least check out the new magazine.

WHERE YOU WILL SPEND YOUR DAY

Web site editors typically work at computers in their own homes. Usually, to benefit from the technological services of a provider, they operate their Web site through a local Internet service provider. Editors determine their own work hours, but must continually be prepared to gather any information that might benefit their online magazines.

CAREER FORECAST

Although increased interest in the Internet may seem to guarantee steady growth in this field, heavy competition creates a high turnover rate.

MONETARY REWARDS

The sole source of income in these sites is the money received from sponsors and advertisers desiring mention in the magazine. Income depends on the subject matter and the potential profit advertisers may realize from buying ad space. Editors must provide their own benefits.

UP THE LADDER

Many editors maintain their magazines as only part-time work because of their lack of success. Successful editors, however, are able to depend fully upon their magazines for financial support. Some may even advance to online entrepreneurship.

From Classroom to . . .

While teaching middle-school English, Sean Brickley became interested in Web site design when he helped his principal put together a Web site for the school. "I loved the challenge of trying new features that added interesting and unique qualities to the Web site. An editor from the local newspaper saw the school's Web site and asked me to help put the newspaper online. As the newspaper's *Web site coordinator and editor,* I meet with department's staff to determine which articles from the hard copy newspaper will be placed online. I then edit the stories to a smaller size and determine which stories will have links to other sections of the online paper or to other Internet sites. In addition to the newspaper Web site editing, I frequently do freelance work for businesses, organizations, churches, and schools in the area."

RELATED JOBS

- Public relations specialist
- Webmaster
- Interior designer and decorator

GATHERING MORE FACTS

Association of Internet Professionals
2629 Main Street #136
Santa Monica, CA 90405
Phone: (609) 737-6842
Internet: www.association.org

Institute for Certification of Computing
    Professionals (ICCP)
2350 East Devon Avenue, Suite 115
Des Plaines, IL 60018

Phone: (800) 843-8227
Internet: www.iccp.org

US Internet Industry Association
919 18th Street, 10th Floor
Washington, DC 20006
Phone: (202) 496-9007
Internet: www.usiia.org

47. *Computer and Video Game Designer*

DEFINITION

Computer and video game designers create the ideas for games played on video consoles, computers, and online Internet subscriptions.

TRANSFERABLE TEACHING SKILLS

- Creativity
- Development skills
- Ability to conceptualize

NECESSARY SKILLS

- Good communication
- Patience
- Technology skills

SUCCESS TIPS

- Know what the public wants
- Have a love of technology
- Conceptualize effectively

9 TO 5: HOW YOU WILL SPEND YOUR DAY

The introduction of computers to the world began a new wave in the entertainment industry—computer games. In just a few decades, computer games have grown to rival most serious business applications in complexity. The people who design these games must quickly go through long, extensive processes to keep the market satisfied with the latest challenges in imagination and problem solving.

Some designers work alone, but most work in complex teams that pool their creativity. These teams begin the design process by identifying their target audience and then define and revise the game's actual design. The design begins as a proposal containing the basic storyline, and this is fleshed out with appearance and sound details, storyline details, and programming tools that create these details. The final design contains the plot and scenes of every section of the game, rules of the game, algorithms, graphic design, audio design, marketing ideas, and even character names. The design of a game can take from six to eighteen months.

WHERE YOU WILL SPEND YOUR DAY

Designers work in office settings that are usually extremely comfortable, so as not to interfere with the design process. Work hours can be very long, sometimes 24 to 48 hours at a time, in order to take advantage of creative spurts. Pressure comes from deadlines, budgets, and design problems.

CAREER FORECAST

Society's obsession with interactive entertainment ensures that this field will continue to grow very quickly.

MONETARY REWARDS

Salaries range from $30,000 to $75,000 per year, although this largely depends upon the location, one's experience, and royalties. Benefits usually include bonuses, vacations, health insurance, and retirement plans.

Up the Ladder

Designers have a variety of advancement options available. Some advance to management positions, while others establish their own gaming companies. Others move to teaching positions or even become authors. The key to advancement is keeping up with current technology.

Related Jobs

- Internet content developer
- Greeting card designer
- Toy and game designer

Gathering More Facts

DigiPen Institute of Technology
5001 15th Avenue, NE
Redmond, WA 98052
Phone: (425) 558-0299
Internet: www.digipen.edu

Gamasutra.com
600 Harrison Street, 2nd Floor
San Francisco, CA 94107
Phone: (415) 947-6000
Internet: www.gamasutra.com

Game Developer
Internet: www.gdmag.com

International Game Developers Association
600 Harrison Street
San Francisco, CA 94107
Phone: (415) 947-6235
Internet: www.igda.org

CHAPTER SEVEN

The Entrepreneur's Life

Many job and career opportunities in the United States can be found in small businesses. One alternative career for teachers is to start their own business. Being a classroom teacher has probably given you some of the necessary skills and abilities. Entrepreneurs must be hard workers, independent, self-starters, self-confident, organized, strong communicators, and most important, creative risk takers. Does this sound like you? Maybe you feel you have what it takes to go out on your own. In this chapter, we'll explore some career ideas for starting your own business.

48. Interior Designer/Decorator

DEFINITION

Interior designers plan the space and furnish the interiors of homes and businesses.

TRANSFERABLE TEACHING SKILLS

- Creativity
- Good listening skills
- Strong communication skills

Necessary Skills

- Detail-orientation
- Knowledge of current fashions and trends
- Many states require licensing

Success Tips

- Learn local codes and laws for buildings
- Appreciate beauty
- Be flexible to the changing styles and tastes of clients

9 to 5: How You Will Spend Your Day

Work may involve the interior of small rooms or the interior of large buildings. Work begins as a process of evaluation. Interior designers and decorators must consider how the space will be used and then use this information to determine how to complete the approved alterations. Designs and decorations are usually presented to the client in formal packages for evaluation. Once approved, designs and decorations must be applied to the space.

Where You Will Spend Your Day

Often, professionals have offices or studios, but most of the work is performed on site, which may be at a home office or other building. Those designers and decorators who work for a company usually log 40-hour weeks, but self-employed professionals have irregular hours in order to work around clients' schedules and meet deadlines.

Career Forecast

As long as the economy does well, interior designers and decorators will be in demand because people have money to create luxurious environments for themselves.

Monetary Rewards

Earnings depend upon experience, clientele, and location. Designer/decorators can earn as much as $250,000 per year, plus benefits.

Up the Ladder

Advancement requires long, tedious training, but it comes in the form of increased income, benefits, and responsibilities.

Related Jobs

- Webmaster
- Web page designer
- Wedding consultant

Gathering More Facts

American Society of Interior Designers
608 Massachusetts Avenue, NE
Washington, DC 20002-6006
Phone: (202) 546-3480
Internet: www.asid.org

Interior Design Educators Council, Inc.
9202 North Meridian Street, Suite 200
Indianapolis, IN 46260-1810
Phone: (317) 816-6261
Internet: www.idec.org

International Interior Design Association
341 Merchandise Mart
Chicago, IL 60654-1104
Phone: (312) 467-1950
Internet: www.iida.com

49. *Small Business Owner*

DEFINITION

Small business owners generally operate a business that has a small number of employees.

TRANSFERABLE TEACHING SKILLS

- Time-management ability
- Critical thinking
- Monitoring
- Instructing

NECESSARY SKILLS

- Must be a competent manager
- Must be familiar with business-related, federal, and state laws
- Must be formally and practically educated in the business

SUCCESS TIPS

- Be willing to take risks
- Be willing to work 12- to 14-hour days
- Be self-motivated

9 TO 5: HOW YOU WILL SPEND YOUR DAY

Small business owners' primary responsibilities are planning, money management, and marketing. Owners must be able to accommodate changing demands and interests of consumers into the products or services being provided. Creative innovation is the key to being a competitive small business owner.

Some owners may have to hire, train, and supervise employees, while other owners may work alone. Often, the owner, with or without employees, must perform other than administrative tasks, such as sales, cleaning, and stocking displays. Small business owners must be prepared to handle every aspect of the business.

WHERE YOU WILL SPEND YOUR DAY

Small business owners work almost entirely at the business location, whether this is a home office or a shop. Owners usually work about 60 to 70 hours a week to ensure that business continues.

CAREER FORECAST

The fastest-growing industries are always filled with small businesses, but the turnover rate of these businesses is high.

MONETARY REWARDS

Earnings depend upon the success of the business. No guaranteed earnings or benefits exist for small business owners. Successful owners know no earning limits.

From Classroom to . . .

Nathan and Janet Michaels *own and operate a small wood furniture and craft store.* Nathan makes almost all of the furniture himself. Janet networks with local artisans and sells their work in the store.

"During my music teaching career, I began making small wood projects like shelves, magazine racks, or table centerpieces. My hobby quickly turned into a full-time occupation. I retired from teaching and now build furniture full time. Janet manages the store. What I like most about my job is taking an idea in my head and creating a beautiful piece of furniture that someone is willing to buy. I've had customers say that my work will be a family heirloom."

Up the Ladder

Advancement is typically only found in the expansion of the business or the expansion of products and services.

Related Jobs

- Store manager
- Property/facility manager
- Advertising/marketing consultant

Gathering More Facts

American Entrepreneur Association
2392 Morse Avenue
Irvine, CA 92714

National Federation of Independent Business
3322 West End Avenue, Suite 700
Nashville, TN 37203
Phone: (800) 634-2669
Internet: www.nfibonline.com

National Retail Federation
325 7th Street, NW, Suite 1100
Washington, DC 20004
Phone: (202) 783-7971
Internet: www.nrf.com

50. *Virtual Office Assistant*

Definition

A virtual office assistant uses computer technology to help businesses complete clerical tasks.

TRANSFERABLE TEACHING SKILLS

- Listening ability
- Time-management
- Information organization

NECESSARY SKILLS

- Must have good word-processing skills
- Must be highly organized
- Must have a marketable, specialized skill, like bookkeeping

SUCCESS TIPS

- Be comfortable using resources found on the Internet
- Meet deadlines
- Be detail-oriented

9 TO 5: HOW YOU WILL SPEND YOUR DAY

Virtual office assistants take advantage of the ease of communication on the Internet to provide administrative services to businesses that do not have the time or resources to perform these tasks on their own. Clients, ranging from entrepreneurs to small companies, hire virtual office assistants through the Internet to perform a variety of tasks, from keeping insurance files updated to planning travel itineraries. Several clients may make simultaneous demands, so organization is essential.

WHERE YOU WILL SPEND YOUR DAY

Virtual office assistants have the advantage of being able to work in any comfortable environment, usually at home with whatever hours they desire. However, prosperous assistants accept any tasks that come their way, so hours depend upon the time demands of clients' requests.

CAREER FORECAST

The outlook is good because of the growth of the Internet and of small businesses.

MONETARY REWARDS

Rates range from $20 to $50 per hour. Depending on the success of the business and number of clients, yearly earnings can range from $25,000 to $80,000.

UP THE LADDER

The only real advancement in this field is the expansion of clientele and benefits.

RELATED JOBS

- Indexer
- Computer trainer
- Paralegal

GATHERING MORE FACTS

International Association of Virtual Office Assistants
Route 1, Box 275
Red Oak, OK 74563
Phone: (918) 753-2716
Internet: www.iavoa.com

International Virtual Assistant Association
17939 Chatsworth Street, Suite 102
Los Angeles, CA 91344
Phone: (877) 440-2750
Internet: www.ivaa.org

The Association of Business Support Services
    International, Inc
5852 Oak Meadow Drive

Yorba Linda, CA 92886-5930
Phone: (714) 695-9398
Internet: www.abssi.org

51. Book Conservators

DEFINITION

Book conservators tend to the pages and bindings of books and nonbook items to preserve authentic artifacts for future use.

TRANSFERABLE TEACHING SKILLS

- Love of books
- Good kinesthetic skills
- Visual skills

NECESSARY SKILLS

- Creative visualization
- Problem-solving
- Fine motor skills

SUCCESS TIPS

- Enjoy working with your hands
- Have an appreciation for history
- Enjoy working alone

9 TO 5: HOW YOU WILL SPEND YOUR DAY

Book conservators treat the bindings and pages of books with chemicals to preserve them, and they often rebind and restitch books to provide fragile pages with new protection from the erosive forces of time. Book conservators work with a variety of old printed materials to preserve recorded history. They repair printed materials that have been damaged by misuse, accident, normal wear and tear, or inferior materials and methods. Such repairs require extensive examination of the damage and a proper diagnosis of the repair method necessary, as defined by knowledge passed down through the history of bookmaking.

All materials that conservators use for repairs must be acid-free, because acidic materials increase decay in printed matter. Repair methods also depend upon the historical and monetary value of the printed matter. Other duties of book conservators depend upon the size of the department in which they operate. These duties may be administrative or educational.

WHERE YOU WILL SPEND YOUR DAY

Most conservators work in climate-controlled, clean areas, out of the path of direct sunlight. These are typically offices in educational departments, where conservators work 40-hour weeks, with regular hours. Work usually is kept within the office environment, although duties not directly related to book conservation may require work elsewhere in the department.

CAREER FORECAST

Book conservation is only a growing field if computer technology is fused with the efforts to preserve information; otherwise, book conservation may actually decline in our digitized society.

MONETARY REWARDS

Depending upon location and range of employment, book conservators may earn from $20,000 to $70,000 a year, with full benefits.

UP THE LADDER

Advancement, in the form of increased administrative responsibility, comes from greater-than-average skill and computer knowledge.

Related Jobs

* Anthropologist
* Records manager
* Painting restorer

Gathering More Facts

American Institute for Conservation of Historic and
    Artistic Works
1717 K Street, NW, Suite 301
Washington, DC 20006
Phone: (202) 452-9545
E-mail: InfoAic@aol.com
Internet: http://palimpsest.Stanford.edu/aic/become/

Foundation of the American Institute for
    Conservation (FAIC)
1717 K Street NW, Suite 301
Washington DC 20006
Phone: (202) 452-9545

Preservation Directorate
Library of Congress
101 Independence Avenue SW
Washington, DC 20540-4320
Phone: (202) 707-5213
E-mail: preserve@loc.gov
Internet: http://cweb.loc.gov/preserve

52. Bed and Breakfast Owners

Definition

Bed and breakfast owners provide meals, keep books and
records, and clean and assign rooms to guests of their establishments.

Transferable Teaching Skills

- Social perceptiveness
- Active listening
- Coordination

Necessary Skills

- Marketing knowledge
- Good business sense
- Comfort with working around people

Success Tips

- Be able to decorate in a pleasing manner
- Manage your time efficiently
- Implement your plans

9 to 5: How You Will Spend Your Day

The owner of a bed and breakfast inn tries to provide guests with a homelike, comfortable environment by taking more active participation in guests' interests than would the owners and operators of a larger hotel or motel. The day begins with the expected homemade breakfast, which should usually accommodate any dietary restrictions the guests may have. After breakfast, the owner works on direct business concerns, particularly reservations.

After guests have left their rooms, owners must clean the rooms, do the laundry, and shop for groceries. Most important, though, are the bed and breakfast owners' efforts to get to know their guests. Guests typically prefer bed and breakfasts over larger hotels because of the personal attention and warmer hospitality of bed and breakfast establishments.

Where You Will Spend Your Day

Bed and breakfast owners are restricted by the nature of their work to their own homes, from which they operate. The envi-

From Classroom to . . .

Gillian and Dan Brooks *own and operate their own bed and breakfast* in a historic house in their town. "Running a bed and breakfast is very hard work. We are responsible for our own marketing, maintenance, cooking, cleaning, and taking care of our guests. While running a bed and breakfast is more risky than the teaching careers we left, we both find tremendous satisfaction in being our own boss."

ronment is generally calm and quiet, with a brief period of hustle during and immediately after breakfast.

CAREER FORECAST

The popularity of bed and breakfasts has increased among vacationers during the past twenty years, but certification and regulations threaten to increase the cost of operating, thus driving up prices and driving away customers.

MONETARY REWARDS

Earnings depend upon location, age, and size. Earnings can range from $25,000 net income a year for a beginning bed and breakfast to $168,000 net income a year for a large, old one.

UP THE LADDER

Advancement is purely in the form of expanding the clientele and the size of the bed and breakfast.

GATHERING MORE FACTS

American Bed and Breakfast Association
1407 Huguenot Road
P.O. Box 1387

Midlothian, VA 23113
Phone: (804) 379-2222
Internet: http://abba.com

Association of Innsitters and Managers
20B Masters Court Drive
New Bern, NC 28562
Phone: (252) 349-5573
Internet: www.aiminnsitter.com

Professional Association of Innkeepers International
P.O. Box 90710
Santa Barbara, CA 93190
Phone: (805) 569-1853
E-mail: info@paii.org
Internet: www.paii.org

53. *Party Planner*

DEFINITION

Party planners conceive, organize, and carry out special functions such as weddings, anniversary parties, or corporate receptions.

TRANSFERABLE TEACHING SKILLS

- Active listening
- Solution appraisal
- Service orientation

NECESSARY SKILLS

- Imagination
- Eye for detail
- Sense of aesthetic design

SUCCESS TIPS

- Be a problem solver
- Manage material resources effectively
- Generate novel ideas

9 TO 5: HOW YOU WILL SPEND YOUR DAY

Party planners begin their work on a special occasion by meeting with clients and determining their specific needs and desires. This meeting focuses on budgeting and creative design. Afterward, party planners usually visit the site of the party to take pictures and measurements, in order to design the best setup for a party at that site. Planners usually assume responsibility for every aspect of the party, from ordering food to supervision of the after-party cleanup.

Party planners, also called party consultants to emphasize their interaction with clients, custom design special events to fit the aesthetic desires, professional needs, and budget limits of the client.

WHERE YOU WILL SPEND YOUR DAY

Party planners usually spend their time either at an event or at their work environment (office, home, or some other place) preparing for an event. Often, because many events take place on weekends, on holidays, and late at night, the party planner must be prepared to forgo regular vacations at these times. Party planners work when everyone else does not.

CAREER FORECAST

As long as the economy doesn't enter a long-term recession, party planning is a growing career, as people desire to celebrate their economic success.

Monetary Rewards

Earnings vary widely; some party planners are salaried, while others are paid from $1,000 to $3,000 per event. Benefits depend upon the employer.

Up the Ladder

Advancement as a party planner will come through experience, advertising, and word of mouth. However, with hard work you will be able to build a bigger business and even expand to include assistants to help satisfy the increased clientele.

Related Jobs

- Artist
- Caterer
- Wedding consultant

Gathering More Facts

Event Solutions Institute
Phone: (800) 529-1101
Internet: www.eventsinstitute.com

International Special Events Society
401 North Michigan Avenue
Chicago, IL 60611-4267
Phone: (800) 688-4737
Internet: www.ises.com

June Wedding, Inc./Association for Event Professionals
1331 Burnham Avenue
Las Vegas, NV 89104-3658
Phone: (702) 474-9558
Internet: www.junewedding.com

54. Caterer

DEFINITION

Caterers prepare, deliver, serve, and sometimes develop themes for customers.

TRANSFERABLE TEACHING SKILLS

- Time management
- Service orientation
- Implementation planning

NECESSARY SKILLS

- Marketing knowledge
- Business sense
- Comfort with working around people

SUCCESS TIPS

- Enjoy working with people
- React quickly to changes
- Have a flair for cooking

9 TO 5: HOW YOU WILL SPEND YOUR DAY

The responsibilities of a caterer vary according to the size of the catering company, but all tasks center upon preparation of food that meets customer demands efficiently and creatively. Caterers hire personnel as needed, provide cooking equipment and menus, and order low-cost, good-quality food. Caterers often must arrange for cleanup after their catered events.

Work hours are at least eight a day, and these are usually irregular hours. Often, caterers must work at night, on weekends, and on holidays, when most special functions take place.

Where You Will Spend Your Day

Caterers spend most work hours on their feet. They may be in the kitchen, delivering goods, servicing social functions, or actively seeking customers. Travel is typically limited to within the caterer's community, although some customers may be located outside city limits.

Career Forecast

Because of higher personal incomes and thriving food industries, demand for catering services should increase as well, thus requiring more caterers.

Monetary Rewards

Earnings depend upon the size and location of the catering business, but owners can earn from $30,000 to $75,000 a year, plus a variety of benefits.

Up the Ladder

Opportunities for advancement come from either the growth of the business, if it is small, or the usual openings created by expansion and retirement in larger catering firms.

Related Jobs

- Baker
- Chef
- Restaurant manager

Gathering More Facts

International Food Service Executives Association
1100 South State Road 7, Suite 103
Margate, FL 33068

From Classroom to . . .

Jerod Thomas can really cook up a storm! He has been *cooking and running his own catering firm* for about three years. In addition to his cooking duties, he must plan the menus for the event, order the food, schedule staff, oversee preparations by the kitchen staff, and coordinate the set-up, serving, and cleanup of the food. Then he completes the paperwork necessary to keep his business running.

"I thoroughly enjoy the challenge of creating unique menu items for the events. Clients want dishes that will make their event memorable." Jerod credits his creativity and success to continuing education courses.

"My goal is to provide very personal service to each of my clients. If they're satisfied with the quality of my service and my food, they'll tell their friends. Word of mouth is my main form of advertisement. The best compliment I can receive after an event is requests for the recipes for the food I serve."

Phone: (954) 977-0767
Internet: www.ifsea.org

Mobile Industrial Caterers Association International
1240 North Jefferson Street, Suite G
Anaheim, CA 92807
Phone: (714) 632-6800

The Educational Foundation of the National Restaurant Association
250 South Wacker Drive, Suite 1400
Chicago, IL 60606
Phone: (800) 765-2122
Internet: www.edfound.org

55. *Personal Chef*

DEFINITION

A personal chef prepares meals for working parents and professionals too busy to prepare their own meals.

TRANSFERABLE TEACHING SKILLS

- Product inspection ability
- Judgment and decision making
- Service orientation

NECESSARY SKILLS

- Cooking talent
- Organization skills
- Eye for detail

SUCCESS TIPS

- Manage your time wisely
- Enjoy working with food
- Cultivate good listening skills

9 TO 5: HOW YOU WILL SPEND YOUR DAY

In a highly technological society that relies on speed and efficiency, many people do not have time or energy to learn how to cook. Some people simply do not have time to cook much at all, even if they know how to cook. Those who grow tired of fast food and microwaved dinners often seek a better alternative, by hiring a personal chef to cook their meals.

Personal chefs shop for all ingredients they need for the meals they prepare, although clients still pay for these purchases. Then, according to the client's dietary needs and menu requests, the personal chef prepares the meals. Usually, these meals are all prepared at the client's home one afternoon each week, and the meals are then packaged with reheating directions attached. Each meal typically contains three or four courses, and a client usually requests from one to ten meals a week. These meals might be for more than one person, as the client could have family or visitors.

Many personal chefs began by cooking for friends, and they simply enjoyed cooking enough to devote all of their time to it. Marketing is the greatest challenge that personal chefs face. Referrals from friends are rarely adequate to build a large-enough clientele. Therefore, many personal chefs utilize brochures, business cards, and media advertisements to attract their clients.

WHERE YOU WILL SPEND YOUR DAY

Personal chefs spend most of their time at their clients' homes, in their kitchens, and at the grocery store. Although they seem to set their own schedules, they must actually arrange for cooking times that are convenient for their clients, which might mean working weekends or evenings.

CAREER FORECAST

The growth of this field, as a newly developing career, is difficult to predict, but there should be some future demand for its services as more and more people enter the workforce.

MONETARY REWARDS

The average salary for a personal chef is about $60,000 a year. The earnings depend upon the rates charged and the number of clients. Usually, the rate is $175 for 10 meals for one client, $275 for ten meals for a couple, and $30 to $50 for each additional person. Personal chefs must provide their own benefits.

UP THE LADDER

Successful personal chefs may be able to expand their businesses to include assistants and, therefore, larger clienteles.

RELATED JOBS

- Butcher
- Caterer
- Industrial baker

GATHERING MORE FACTS

American Culinary Federation
P.O. Box 3466
St. Augustine, FL 32085

International Association of Culinary Professionals (IACP)
304 West Liberty Street, Suite 201
Louisville, KY 40202
Phone: (502) 581-9786
Internet: www.iacp.com

United States Personal Chef Association (USPCA)
481 Rio Rancho Boulevard, NE
Rio Rancho, New Mexico 87124
Phone: (800) 995-2138
Internet: www.uspca.com

56. *Pet Sitter*

DEFINITION

Pet sitters take care of people's pets when owners are on vacation or are working long hours.

TRANSFERABLE TEACHING SKILLS

- Time management
- Critical thinking
- Judgment and decision making

NECESSARY SKILLS

- Love of animals
- Self-motivation
- Dependability

SUCCESS TIPS

- Be trustworthy
- Be organized
- Be reliable

9 TO 5: HOW YOU WILL SPEND YOUR DAY

Pet sitting is a hobby for some people, but others have made a lucrative career out of it. Enough people cannot stand to leave their pets at kennels or boarders to provide pet sitters with plenty of business. Using a pet sitter allows pets to stay in familiar surroundings and avoids health risks presented by contact with other animals, such as in a kennel. Hiring a pet sitter also guarantees regular exercise and diet for pets.

Pet sitters may be called upon to take care of a variety of animals, from cats and dogs to fish and gerbils. Pet sitters are given their own set of keys by their clients so that they may care for pets in the animals' own homes. Pet sitters feed, water, and medicate the animals when necessary. They clean the pets' litter boxes and any messes the animals have made. Sitters play with the animals, let them outside, and take them for walks. Pet sitters often offer a variety of services to their clients, such as veterinarian visits, grooming, and pet-related products.

Pet sitters work alone most of the time, making one to three 30- to 60-minute visits to each client's home each day agreed upon. At times, they may even spend the night at a client's house. Pet sitters also take care of clients' homes by bringing in mail, watering plants, and securing exits.

Where You Will Spend Your Day

Work hours are entirely planned around client schedules, so it is difficult for sitters to set up specific routines. The environment of the pet sitter varies from house to house, but much time may be spent outdoors, even in inclement weather, to allow pets their exercise.

Career Forecast

Because of the cost-effectiveness and desirability of a pet sitter's services in comparison to alternatives, this field should grow very quickly.

Monetary Rewards

Salaries can range from $5,000 to $100,000 a year. Benefits are the responsibility of the pet sitter. The salary range is so great that no average can be determined. Salaries depend upon the rates charged, the location of the sitter, and the number of clients taken. Pet sitters in large cities typically earn more than those in smaller towns.

Up the Ladder

Advancement is in the form of a larger clientele or even an assistant. Some pet sitters are so successful that they develop large operations, even franchises, with entire staffs.

Related Jobs

- Animal trainer
- Rancher
- Veterinary technician

Gathering More Facts

National Federation of Independent Business
3322 West End Avenue, Suite 700
Nashville, TN 37203

Phone: (800) 634-2669
Internet: www.nfibonline.com

Pet Sitters International
201 East King Street
King, NC 27021-9163
Phone: (336) 983-9222
Internet: www.petsit.com

National Association of Professional Pet Sitters
6 State Road, Suite 113
Mechanicburg, PA 17050
Phone: (717) 691-5565
Internet: www.petsitters.org

57. *Wedding Consultant*

DEFINITION

Wedding consultants assist in the planning of weddings.

TRANSFERABLE TEACHING SKILLS

* Implementation planning
* Coordination
* Active listening

NECESSARY SKILLS

* Patience
* Creativity
* Excellent people skills

SUCCESS TIPS

* Be able to steer clients in the right direction
* Work within the client's budget
* Be flexible

9 to 5: How You Will Spend Your Day

The average wedding costs nearly $20,000, but many brides only become frustrated with their weddings. In recent years, wedding consultants have become an accepted, even necessary, part of weddings. Wedding consultants primarily help brides avoid the stress of planning every detail by assisting them from the earliest stages on forward. Occasionally, consultants may only be requested to help in certain stages, but they typically are involved in the entire planning process.

Wedding consultants often receive discounts on vendor's services because they bring additional business that those vendors would not otherwise receive. These savings are usually passed on to the clients. Often, a consultant will accompany the client on visits to vendors in order to negotiate prices. Consultants usually have particular vendors whom they recommend for particular services because of good prices and quality of service. Consultants also arrange for wedding sites, order invitations, and find desired music.

Consultants advise clients on wedding traditions and etiquette and help clients determine the specifics of unusual wedding additions, such as having butterflies released at the wedding. Consultants are busy throughout the ceremony and the reception, making sure that everything runs smoothly and handling emergencies.

Where You Will Spend Your Day

During the week, wedding consultants meet vendors, take phone calls at home or the office, and make plans, perhaps with the aid of a computer. Some consultants have business offices, but many operate out of their own homes. Their weekends and evenings are occupied with attending the weddings and receptions they have planned with their clients.

Career Forecast

The increase in sophisticated weddings and anniversary vow renewals ensures that this career will grow some in the future.

Monetary Rewards

Initial consultation fees range from $275 to $425 for about three hours. Pre-wedding planning fees range from $1,000 to $2,000, while wedding day fees range from $1,200 to $1,800. In large cities, wedding consultants can expect to have a wedding planned for each weekend. Consultants must provide their own benefits.

Up the Ladder

Advancement comes through experience and consists of building a bigger business. Advanced consultants can afford to hire a regular staff and expand their services to maintain Web sites, provide special invitations, and so on.

Related Jobs

- Bed and breakfast owner
- Florist
- Hotel concierge

Gathering More Facts

Association of Bridal Consultants
200 Chestnutland Road
New Milford, Connecticut 06776-2521
Phone: (860) 355-0464
Internet: www.bridalassn.com

June Wedding, Inc.
1331 Burnham Avenue
Las Vegas, NV 89104-3658
Phone: (792) 474-9558
Internet: hwww.junewedding.com

National Bridal Service
3122 West Cary Street
Richmond, VA 23221

Phone: (804) 355-6945
Internet: www.nationalbridalservice.com

58. *Personal Shopper*

DEFINITION

Personal shoppers search various shopping sources for the best available items for their clients.

TRANSFERABLE TEACHING SKILLS

- Recommending
- Serving
- Selecting

NECESSARY SKILLS

- Creativity
- Active listening
- Honesty (with clients about purchases)

SUCCESS TIPS

- Stay aware of current fashion
- Have a personal flair for style
- Cultivate good people skills

9 TO 5: HOW YOU WILL SPEND YOUR DAY

Personal shoppers are responsible for determining what customers want and obtaining the information needed to serve them. Shoppers accomplish this by sending catalogs and browsing the Internet and stores for that "special something."

Personal shoppers may buy anything for clients, depending on the clients' needs and the expertise of the shopper. Personal shoppers are essentially looked upon to produce the perfect gift and to offer valuable advice for their clients. They help professionals design exciting wardrobes, while relying on their keen knowledge of the local marketplace to complete the shopping as quickly and efficiently as possible.

As a personal shopper, you will visit your client's home and evaluate your client's wardrobe. At this point, the client and the shopper decide what direction the client's wardrobe will take. The shopper also advises the client on how to mix and match the new wardrobe. Personal shoppers may be required to shop for gifts, schedule appointments, keep records, and make phone calls for their clients.

WHERE YOU WILL SPEND YOUR DAY

Because you work for yourself, you have the luxury of setting your own work hours. Most personal shoppers work from their homes. Much of their time will be spent in clients' homes and going to department stores.

CAREER FORECAST

There isn't much information available to predict how this field will progress. With the advent of online shopping, personal shoppers will either lose or gain access to many "potential" clients in need of personal assistance. Personal shoppers need to make themselves marketable by offering as many services as possible.

MONETARY REWARDS

Personal shoppers bill clients in various ways. Some charge an hourly rate, while others use a regular fee for services rendered. For hourly rates, shoppers generally charge between $25 and $125, with the average being about $75. Shoppers in large metropolitan areas may make anywhere from $1,500 to $3,000 a month. Ultimately, your yearly earnings depend greatly on your method of billing and your geographical location.

Up the Ladder

Personal shoppers must be persistent to advance in this field. Advertising is critical to your success. As your reputation grows, so will your clientele.

Related Jobs

- Professional organizer
- Retail manager
- Wedding planner

Gathering More Facts

National Association of Professional Organizers
1033 La Posada, Suite 220
Austin, TX 78752

From Classroom to . . .

Wow! Shopping as a career! Ann Marie Sanchez feels she has found her dream career. She didn't need any additional training for this new job and was very happy to leave the classroom. "I'm still able to use the communication skills I used as a teacher with my junior high social studies students. I enjoy knowing that I'm helping to make my customers' lives easier." As a *personal shopper,* Ann Marie must be aware of every item a store sells and know what department each item is located in. Similar to when she was department chair of the social studies department, Ann Marie has the opportunity to work with other employees throughout the store.

"Best of all, I enjoy being able to move freely around the store and set my own schedule. It's very satisfying to see the look on a client's face when she sees an item that's exactly what she wants."

Phone: (512) 206-0151
Internet: www.napolnet

Personal Assistants International
1800 30th Street, Suite 220C
Boulder, CO 80301
Phone: (303) 443-7646
Internet: www.personalassistants.com

Professional Organizers Web Ring
Internet: www.organizerswebring.com

59. *Internet Entrepreneur*

DEFINITION

An Internet entrepreneur applies marketing and sales knowledge to sell products and services by way of the Internet.

TRANSFERABLE TEACHING SKILLS

- Ability to develop ideas
- Computer literacy
- Motivating skills

NECESSARY SKILLS

- Dedication
- Good communication
- Marketing skills

SUCCESS TIPS

- Be a risk-taker
- Have a good sense of design
- Conceptualize and implement your ideas effectively

9 TO 5: HOW YOU WILL SPEND YOUR DAY

The growth of the Internet in the past thirty years has provided businesses and entrepreneurs with more global, less expensive means of communicating with potential consumers than were previously available. The Internet has allowed us to communicate as intricately as our economy and our environment are connected. Entrepreneurs are just some of the people who have taken advantage of this globalization; they use a combination of marketing techniques, valuable products or services, and knowledge of the Internet to sell goods and services to the world.

Two types of commercial Web sites exist through which entrepreneurs provide connection to consumers—pay sites and free sites. Free sites attempt to attract consumers with useful or interesting information, earning money by soliciting visitors to purchase advertised goods or by allowing other businesses to advertise for a fee. Pay sites require consumers to pay to view the site's information. Pay sites have free sections that solicit paying consumers, who are then provided with a variety of passwords or identification numbers to access the restricted information.

WHERE YOU WILL SPEND YOUR DAY

Entrepreneurs usually work at home, although some are employed by companies and work in pleasant, dust-free offices, work hours are typically determined by each entrepreneur, although successful entrepreneurship requires long, stressful hours.

CAREER FORECAST

Although the growth of the Internet would seem to imply growth in this field, the overabundance of information available on the Internet requires much work to overcome the high turnover rate and heavy competition.

MONETARY REWARDS

Most Internet entrepreneurs only make $600 to $1,300 per week before subtracting operation costs, although some may make as much as $250,000 per year. Those employed by businesses typically receive benefits, including vacations, health insurance, and unemployment insurance. Self-employment entrepreneurs must provide their own benefits.

UP THE LADDER

Advancement consists of developing a successful Web site, the success of which is determined by the steadiness of its "hits," or visitors. Entrepreneurs who do not receive enough "hits" usually cannot afford to maintain their sites for long.

RELATED JOBS

- Bed and breakfast owner
- Greeting card designer
- Internet content developer

GATHERING MORE FACTS

Association of On-Line Professionals
6096 Franconia Road, Suite D
Alexandria, VA 22310
Phone: (703) 924-5800
Internet: www.aop.org

Internet Society
12020 Sunrise Valley Drive, Suite 210
Reston, VA 22091
Phone: (703) 648-9888
Internet: www.isoc.org

Interpreneur.com
Internet: http://interpreneur.com

And Now for Something Completely Different

Hey! If you're just looking for a change, this is the chapter for you. If you haven't yet decided what field to get into, but know that you want a change from teaching, these jobs offer a way to earn a living and leave the classroom behind.

Have you ever thought of working in the toy industry or breeding small animals? Maybe you're creative and would like to design greeting cards. Could you help people get organized? If this sounds like you, then read this chapter about some unusual, but interesting, careers.

60. *Paralegal*

DEFINITION

Paralegals, or legal assistants, perform a variety of routine legal activities normally done by lawyers.

Transferable Teaching Skills

- Written comprehension skills
- Information ordering skills
- Computer skills

Necessary Skills

- Ability to do research
- Interviewing skills
- Investigative talent

Success Tips

- Handle routine assignments efficiently
- Handle the pressures of deadlines in a calm manner
- Be able to search out information

9 to 5: How You Will Spend Your Day

Lawyers, with their increasing caseloads, often do not have time to complete a variety of mundane, but necessary, tasks. Paralegals perform these tasks for them. Lawyers assume responsibility for their paralegals' work, which may be any of the average lawyer's duties except setting fees, court appearances, case acceptance, and giving legal advice.

Paralegals typically work in law libraries, where they research laws and cases to help lawyers prepare for trials. Paralegals may also interview witnesses, prepare legal arguments, and organize and store case files. Usually, paralegals compile all information and suggestions into reports for their lawyers.

Some paralegals work for schools, agencies, corporations, and financial institutions. These paralegals focus on creating and maintaining their employers' financial and legal documents, such as contracts, mortgages, and affidavits. Corporate paralegals assist in shareholder matters, such as agreements and contracts, and keep their companies aware of new laws and regulations affecting business.

WHERE YOU WILL SPEND YOUR DAY

Most paralegals work in pleasant office environments, usually law libraries. Travel for investigative purposes is sometimes an option. Most paralegals work forty hours a week. Overtime may be necessary to meet court deadlines or to become oriented in a new position in a firm.

CAREER FORECAST

Economic growth and the cost-effectiveness of paralegal services have made this field one of the fastest-growing occupations in the industry. There will be a lot of competition for open positions. Law firms will continue to be the largest employers of paralegals, but other organizations, such as insurance companies, banks, real estate firms, and large corporate legal departments, will need more paralegals.

MONETARY REWARDS

Salary depends upon the size and location of the employer, as well as on the education and experience of the paralegal. Salaries range from $23,800 to $50,000 a year, with potential year-end bonuses and excellent benefits—vacation time, retirement plans, and insurance.

UP THE LADDER

Advancement comes through experience or specialization. Some paralegals obtain supervisory or specialized positions, while others move into larger firms. Some paralegals even begin their own freelance businesses. Others move into related fields or go to law school.

RELATED JOBS

- Claim examiner
- Patent agent
- Title examiner

From Classroom to . . .

Paralegal Kelly O'Neil decided to take some classes on the side after her daily elementary teaching job was finished. She enrolled in the American Bar Association Certified Paralegal Program at the local business college. It took almost two years of study to become certified. Although not all *paralegal* positions require certification, Kelly felt that it would help her gain employment when she left the teaching profession.

"Today the tasks I handle are very different from writing report cards, teaching daily spelling words, and grading homework. Now I interview potential clients, summarize depositions, research documents at the federal courthouse, assist with trial procedures, and obtain expert witnesses. I love the change and the new challenges."

GATHERING MORE FACTS

National Association of Legal Assistants, Inc
1516 South Boston Street, Suite 200
Tulsa, OK 74119
Phone: (918) 587-6828
Internet: www.nala.org

National Federation of Paralegal Associations
P.O. Box 33108
Kansas City, MO 64114-0108
Phone: (816) 941-4000
Internet: www.paralegals.org

National Paralegal Association
P.O. Box 406
Solebury, PA 18963
Phone: (215) 297-8333
Internet: www.nationalparalegal.org

61. *Museum Curator*

DEFINITION

Museum curators create museum exhibits and manage the work of museums.

TRANSFERABLE TEACHING SKILLS

- Instructing
- Envisioning
- Organizing

NECESSARY SKILLS

- Creativity
- Speaking
- Information gathering

SUCCESS TIPS

- Be able to communicate information so that others will clearly understand
- Know how to find and identify essential information
- Have a genuine love of history

9 TO 5: HOW YOU WILL SPEND YOUR DAY

A variety of museums exist, but all of their curators must perform similar duties. Museum curators design, oversee, and install new exhibits. At times, curators have a particularly useful talent in the maintenance and/or display of exhibits; they may temporarily travel with exhibits if they are shown at more than one museum. Curators also modify or add to current exhibits. They organize gallery talks and educational programs. Curators continuously search for new items to add to existing exhibits or to collect for future exhibits.

    Once new items are discovered, curators work within the museum's budget to acquire these items. Acquired items are catalogued and sometimes restored to display quality. All items, whether stored or exhibited, must be carefully maintained to prevent decay.

One type of curator, an operation worker, is the supervisor of the entire museum. This person oversees all routine tasks and functions of the museum, such as budgeting, maintenance, security, admissions, and so on.

WHERE YOU WILL SPEND YOUR DAY

Most curators can be found in major cities, such as New York, Chicago, Washington, and Boston—where the largest museums are located. Curators typically work 40-hour weeks within a museum, although those in charge of locating new items for exhibits may be required to travel to find rare items.

CAREER FORECAST

The lack of museum growth and the increased computerization of item location have slowed the growth of this field. There are more qualified individuals than job openings. Thus competition for these jobs is high.

MONETARY REWARDS

Curators earn from $22,000 to $45,000 a year. Salaries depend largely upon their education level and museum experience. Benefits vary widely, depending upon the size of the museum and the title of the curator.

UP THE LADDER

Advancement is slow, but is typically through educational improvement and work experience. Supervisory positions are usually the available forms of advancement.

RELATED JOBS

- Anthropologist
- Historian
- Records manager

GATHERING MORE FACTS

Advisory Council on Historic Preservation
1100 Pennsylvania Avenue, NW, Suite 809
Washington, DC 20004
Phone: (202) 606-8507
Internet: www.achp.gov

American Association of Museums
1575 I Street, NW, Suite 400
Washington, DC 20005
Phone: (202) 289-1818
Internet: www.aam-us.org

The Society of American Archivists
527 South Wells Street, 5th Floor
Chicago, IL 60607-3922
Phone: (312) 922-0140
Internet: www.archivists.org

62. *Lobbyist*

DEFINITION

Lobbyists try to influence government legislation to benefit their clients.

TRANSFERABLE TEACHING SKILLS

- Speaking skills
- Social perceptiveness
- Persuasiveness

NECESSARY SKILLS

- Honesty
- Good communication
- Negotiating skills

SUCCESS TIPS

- Be aware of others' reactions
- Motivate people
- Reorganize information to get a better approach to the problems

9 TO 5: HOW YOU WILL SPEND YOUR DAY

Nonprofit organizations, labor unions, trade associations, corporations, and other groups usually employ lobbyists. Lobbyists utilize legislative insights and contacts to voice their clients' concerns and opinions. Most lobbyists can be found in Washington, D.C.

Lobbyists represent their clients' interests through one or both of these techniques: direct lobbying and indirect, or grass roots, lobbying. Direct lobbying techniques make use of personal contacts in key government positions, such as Congress. Lobbyists must keep track of the people who influence legislation in which clients have an interest. Then they gather information that is favorable to their clients' interests and make certain that legislators obtain and review this information. In this way, lobbyists attempt to directly sway legislative opinion in favor of their clients' interests.

Indirect, or grassroots, lobbying attempts to evoke a strong voter reaction in favor of client interests, thus driving elected officials to side with their constituencies in an effort to stay popular in future elections. Grassroots lobbying bombards voters through various means of communication, such as mail, phone calls, and media, until voters voice their opinions enough to affect legislation in favor of client interests.

WHERE YOU WILL SPEND YOUR DAY

Corporate lobbyists typically reside in Washington, D.C., while lobbyists in lobby firms may be located across the country. The environment of lobbyists remains varied, as they must consistently stay aware of current issues and trends, gather information, meet with legislators, and attend meetings. Work hours are often irregular.

CAREER FORECAST

Because of the steady growth of special interest groups, lobbyists are in constant demand.

From Classroom to . . .

Marcus Baxter is a principal for a two-man lobbying firm located near Washington, D.C. His background in education as a teacher, assistant principal, and principal was a valuable building block to his career as a *lobbyist*.

"A lobbyist must have excellent speaking and communication skills in order to influence officials within the government. However, before a lobbyist speaks, he must listen carefully to the goals and objectives of the person or organization he is lobbying. For a lobbyist to accomplish his goals, he must work to help the person or organization accomplish their goals. Diplomacy is a key ingredient to getting things accomplished in government.

"As a school principal, I was responsible for overseeing the classroom teachers who implemented the curriculum set forth by the state and local school boards. It was sometimes necessary to negotiate with the teachers and persuade them of the value of a new program or curriculum. Creating a situation in which teachers felt they were gaining something often resulted in a smooth, successful implementation. It was important to develop a win-win environment."

Monetary Rewards

Salaries for lobbyists range from $20,000 to $700,000 a year, depending upon the size of the clientele. Employers may offer benefits, but lobbyists usually must provide their own benefits.

Up the Ladder

Advancement depends upon successful, trustworthy experience with legislators. Corporate lobbyists may advance to higher executive positions, while lobbying firm lobbyists advance by taking on more clients.

Related Jobs

- Congressional aide
- Political scientist
- Speech writer

Gathering More Facts

American League of Lobbyists
P.O. Box 30005
Alexandria, VA 22310
Phone: (703) 960-3011
Internet: www.alldc.org

American Society of Association Executives
1575 I Street, NW
Washington, DC 20005
Phone: (202) 626-2723
Internet: www.asaenet.org

Public Affairs Council
2033 K Street, NW, Suite 700
Washington, DC 20006
Phone: (202) 872-1790
Internet: www.pac.org

63. *Professional Speaker*

DEFINITION

Professional speakers speak to an audience on a topic of interest, such as self-improvement, sales/marketing, or educational issues.

TRANSFERABLE TEACHING SKILLS

- Organizational skills
- Time management
- Critical thinking

NECESSARY SKILLS

- Speaking skills
- Information-gathering ability
- Interpersonal skills

SUCCESS TIPS

- Use good marketing techniques
- Negotiate skillfully
- Use multiple teaching approaches

9 TO 5: HOW YOU WILL SPEND YOUR DAY

Professional speakers are hired to speak for conferences, conventions, colleges, seminar companies, corporations, nonprofit organizations, and even cruise ships. Professional speakers can choose from innumerable topics, including organization, time management, nonverbal communication, stress management, and sales techniques. Topics can be education-based, such as managing a classroom; building children's self-esteem; helping children succeed in the classroom; communicating with parents, colleagues, and supervisors; teaching techniques for any subject area; and even bringing humor into the classroom. Personal experiences, overcoming life's challenges, and motivational speeches are marketable topics for professional speakers.

Professional speakers fall into two main categories: independent speakers or those contracting through speakers' bureaus or other speakers' firms. Independent speakers are responsible for developing their own topics and negotiating a fee and contract, as well as for making travel and lodging arrangements. They often create and market their own products, such as audio or videotapes, books, or CDs that supplement and reinforce their speaking topic.

Marketing themselves is probably the most time-consuming, challenging, and cost-intensive aspect of the independent speaker's career. Making "cold calls" is one marketing technique, in which speakers call people or organizations that may be interested in their services. Referrals from audience members, family, friends, colleagues, and acquaintances may give the speaker leads to more engagements. Many professional speakers use the media to promote themselves. They appear on radio, television, and in print to give advice in their area of expertise. They may also use the Internet and e-mail to market themselves and their products. Independent speakers either handle all arrangements and marketing for themselves or have a staff to do so.

Professional speakers may contract through a speaking bureau or a professional speakers' firm. In this case, the bureau or firm handles all arrangements, fees, contracts, and even product inventory. The bureau or firm keeps a portion of the speaker's fee as payment for its services. The advantage of using a bureau or firm is that speakers can focus their time on speechwriting, developing new topics, and tailoring a presentation to a client's specific needs. The disadvantage may be a lower net fee for each speaking engagement than if the speaker had solicited and contracted directly with a client.

WHERE YOU WILL SPEND YOUR DAY

Professional speakers spend a lot of time traveling to and from speaking engagements. When not speaking or traveling, they may work in an office, often located in their home. Work hours vary greatly and depend on when the client has scheduled conventions, seminars, workshops, and so on.

Career Forecast

There is rapid expansion in the meeting and convention industry, as well as in the professional speaking profession. Professional speakers are in demand by all types of industries because they can be the catalyst for improving productivity, increasing sales, and helping employees have better, healthier lives.

Monetary Rewards

Earnings for professional speakers vary widely. The average fee paid for speakers at convention general sessions and general meetings is $3,500. For educational seminars, speakers earn an average of $1,500 per engagement. The annual earnings depend on the number of engagements the speaker books. The sale of educational materials, books, videos, tapes, and CDs can supplement a professional speaker's annual earnings.

Up the Ladder

Advancement for professional speakers typically comes from booking more speaking engagements and negotiating higher speaking fees. Individuals contracting with speakers' bureaus or firms may become independent speakers or contract with multiple bureaus or firms.

Related Jobs

- Advertising/marketing consultant
- Sales representative
- Small business owner

GATHERING MORE FACTS

Advanced Public Speaking Institute
Box 2630
Landover Hills, MD 20784
Phone: (800) 752-4611
Internet: www.public-speaking.org

American Speakers Bureau Corporation
10151 University Boulevard #197
Orlando, Florida 32817
Phone: (407) 826-4248
Internet: www.speakersbureau.com

National Speakers Association
1500 South Priest Drive
Tempe, AZ 85281
Phone: (480) 968-2552
Internet: www.nsaspeaker.org

Toastmasters International
P.O. Box 9052
Mission Viejo, CA 92690-7052
Phone: (949) 858-8255
Internet: http://www.toastmasters.org

64. *Demographer*

DEFINITION

Demographers gather and analyze statistical data on human
population changes, trends, and movements.

TRANSFERABLE TEACHING SKILLS

- Analyzing statistical data
- Ability to read charts and graphs
- Information gathering

Necessary Skills

- Mathematical ability
- Problem-solving skills
- Good communication

Success Tips

- Evaluate outcomes
- Identify essential information
- Have a good background in mathematics

9 to 5: How You Will Spend Your Day

A demographer takes population data, often from a national census or a poll, and organizes it in a statistical format for analysis. This format varies, depending upon the analysis required and the conclusions desired. Graphs, charts, and frequency tables are often used to clearly show trends and changes.

Most demographers use a technique called sampling: recording the characteristics of a part, or sample, of a target population. This data is assumed to be representative of the entire population. The samples may come from government surveys, private surveys, and public opinion polls, as well as from the demographer's employer.

Employers of demographers include the government, which needs social science issues settled, such as illness rates, health services, crime rates, and so on. Private companies also employ demographers in order to make marketing decisions based on trend projections. Demographers typically either perform long-range planning or teach. Demographers employed by various companies and government branches aid them in setting long-term goals, while demographers in universities serve as consultants and teachers.

Where You Will Spend Your Day

Demographers work in pleasant offices or classrooms. Travel is occasionally an option, to attend a conference or perform field research. Demographers typically work 40-hour weeks, although overtime may be necessary to meet a project deadline.

CAREER FORECAST

Growth in this field will be rather slow, and only the most highly educated will be selected in this very competitive field.

MONETARY REWARDS

Salaries depend upon education level and location of employment. Salaries range from $19,500 to $66,000 a year. Benefits include annual vacations, group insurance, and a retirement plan.

UP THE LADDER

Advancement comes through specialization in an accepted area of interest, such as education or health services; the continuance of education; or both. The higher the level of education, the more likely you will get promoted.

RELATED JOBS

- Computer programmer
- Mathematician
- Statistician

GATHERING MORE FACTS

American Sociological Association
1307 New York Avenue, NW, Suite 700
Washington, DC 20005
Phone: (202) 383-9005
Internet: www.asanet.org

Association of Population Centers
Internet: www.popcenters.org

Population Association of America
8630 Fenton Street, Suite 722
Silver Spring, MD 20910-3812
Phone: (301) 565-6710
Internet: www.popassoc.org

65. *Actuary*

DEFINITION

Actuaries gather, organize, and analyze data to estimate the probabilities of death, illness, injury, disability, and property losses, in order to set a policy for insurance and pension plans.

TRANSFERABLE TEACHING SKILLS

- Organizational ability
- Interpersonal skills
- Critical thinking

NECESSARY SKILLS

- Strong math background
- Ability to do research
- Decision-making skills

SUCCESS TIPS

- Keep up with your continuing education
- Be detail-oriented
- Be logical

9 TO 5: HOW YOU WILL SPEND YOUR DAY

Many actuaries work with property and casualty or life and health insurance firms. Others work in pension planning, investment, or risk classification with banks, investment firms, and the government.

Actuaries who work with insurance companies gather and analyze statistics in areas such as auto accidents, death, illness, and injury. They look at age, driving patterns, car costs, and property values. All of this information helps the insurance company determine policy rates so that it is able to pay claims and other expenses, yet still make a profit and remain competitive with other insurance companies.

Actuaries working within the financial industry help determine prices for investment options. They also help manage credit issues for the bank. Pension actuaries evaluate pension plans to determine risks and soundness.

Some actuaries work on contract with clients. These actuaries provide short-term advice to insurance companies, corporations, health maintenance organizations, government agencies, and attorneys. Consulting actuaries may testify in court for people who have been disabled or killed in an accident. The actuary testifies to the client's potential lifetime earnings in an effort to recover damage awards for the client.

WHERE YOU WILL SPEND YOUR DAY

Actuaries usually have comfortable offices and work forty hours per week. Overtime and travel may be required, especially for consulting actuaries, who need to meet with clients. Actuary jobs are concentrated in cities with prominent financial districts.

CAREER FORECAST

Job opportunities for actuaries will likely increase in the health insurance and the property/casualty fields. Some companies may downsize or merge with other firms, causing a slower than average growth. Employment opportunities will be best for consulting actuaries, as more firms look to short-term contracts as a way to control costs. This trend will be most prevalent in investment firms and large corporations.

MONETARY REWARDS

The average annual earnings for actuaries are $65,500. Starting actuaries earn about $37,000 per year, while the top earners make nearly $124,000 per year. Actuaries employed by the federal government earn an average of $73,000 per year. Benefits vary with the employer, but typically include health and life insurance, vacation and sick leave, as well as pension plans.

UP THE LADDER

Advancement depends on job performance and the number of actuarial examinations passed. Those with more knowledge in a range of fields have better opportunities for advancement to supervisory or managerial positions. Some actuaries take up teaching positions at colleges or universities offering actuarial studies.

RELATED JOBS

- Insurance agent
- Financial planner
- Real estate appraiser

GATHERING MORE FACTS

American Society of Pension Actuaries
4245 North Fairfax Drive, Suite 750
Arlington, VA 22203
Phone: (703) 516-9300
Internet: www.aspa.org

Casualty Actuarial Society
1100 North Glebe Road, Suite 600
Arlington, VA 22201
Phone: (703) 276-3100
Internet: www.casact.org

Society of Actuaries
475 North Martingale Road, Suite 800
Schaumburg, IL 60173-2226
Phone: (847) 706-3500
Internet: www.soa.org.

66. *Real Estate Appraiser*

DEFINITION

A real estate appraiser determines the value of buildings and land.

TRANSFERABLE TEACHING SKILLS

- Estimating
- Math skills
- Precision

NECESSARY SKILLS

- Mathematical background
- Evaluating
- Interviewing

SUCCESS TIPS

- Enjoy working in different locations
- Be able to write reports
- Have good calculating skills

9 TO 5: HOW YOU WILL SPEND YOUR DAY

Real estate always has a changing value that is used for sales, investments, loans, and mortgages. Real estate appraisers determine this value through an appraisal process. This value is an estimate of the amount the property should properly be sold for under current market conditions.

The appraisal process involves visiting the property, measuring it, interviewing people familiar with it, and inspecting its design condition and construction. Appraisers then consider location, buying trends, and local real estate transactions. Standard valuing formulas are also used.

After this information is gathered, a real estate appraiser creates an appraisal report. This is a written description of the legal and physical aspects of the property, with the appraiser's estimate of its value. The report contains photographs of the property, pertinent blueprints, and a detailed explanation of the appraiser's valuation process.

Real estate appraisers may choose to specialize in appraising a particular type of real estate, such as commercial, residential, agricultural, or rental property. Specialization often depends upon the appraiser's employer. Some appraisers work for private corporations or financial institutions, while others work in private firms.

WHERE YOU WILL SPEND YOUR DAY

Real estate appraisers spend part of their time in pleasant offices completing paperwork. The rest is spent performing on-site investigations of property and in meetings with buyers and sellers. Appraisers often work more than forty hours a week because of appointments with people concerned about the property in question.

CAREER FORECAST

Growth in this highly competitive field is much slower than average.

MONETARY REWARDS

Salaries range from $17,000 to $65,000 a year, depending upon the number of appraisals performed. Benefits for corporate appraisers include vacations, insurance plans, and pension plans.

From Classroom to . . .

"I've always enjoyed the outdoors. As a second-grade teacher, I spent almost my entire day inside the school. When I became restless and dissatisfied with my teaching position, my husband, a realtor, suggested that I look into real estate appraisal. It wasn't long before I was working out of his office as an independent appraiser. I find that I have more flexibility in my schedule so that I can be more involved in my children's activities."

—JESSICA KIEFER, *independent real estate appraiser*

UP THE LADDER

Real estate appraisers advance either through experience or specialization. Some become senior appraisers, while others find job security and advancement in specializing in the appraisal of particular types of property.

RELATED JOBS

- Antique valuation
- Insurance agent
- Securities and financial services

GATHERING MORE FACTS

American Society of Appraisers
555 Herndon Parkway, Suite 125
Herndon, VA 20170
Phone: (703) 478-2228
Internet: www.appraisers.org

Real Estate Educators Association
320 West Sabal Palm Place, Suite 150
Longwood, FL 32779

Phone: (407) 834-6688
Internet: www.reea.org

Realtors Land Institute
430 North Michigan Avenue
Chicago, IL 60611
Phone: (312) 329-8440

67. *Professional Organizer*

DEFINITION

Professional organizers help people organize and effectively manage their lives.

TRANSFERABLE TEACHING SKILLS

- Good listening skills
- Ascertaining
- Classifying

NECESSARY SKILLS

- Organizational skills
- Time management
- Good communication

SUCCESS TIPS

- Be able to work well with people
- Consolidate what is needed
- Eliminate the unnecessary

9 TO 5: HOW YOU WILL SPEND YOUR DAY

The most difficult work a professional organizer will ever have to perform is attracting clients. Most professional organizers begin small, through a number of methods. Some start by helping neighbors organize their homes and schedules. From this simple beginning, professional organizers allow their skills to spread by word of mouth. Some professional organizers teach time-management classes to small groups at a community center or an adult education program, while others teach similar classes at home. Some publish brief newsletters with advice and send them to local businesses as examples of their skills. Some arrange for speaking engagements at business organization meetings, receptions, or conferences. All of these techniques are geared toward galvanizing disorganized people's interest in the skills of a professional organizer.

When professional organizers are hired, they examine the client's life through interviews and observations of the client's environment. After a clear goal is agreed upon, the professional organizer helps the client implement organizational and time-management techniques.

WHERE YOU WILL SPEND YOUR DAY

Although some promotional work may be done at home, organizers typically spend most of their time on others' prop-

From Classroom to . . .

"Friends and colleagues always said I was a very organized person. I guess I was born with that special organizing gene. Even while growing up, I looked for ways to keep things organized."

Nancy Caswell was a first-grade teacher before starting her own organizing business. "I taught school for only two years before I was let go because of low enrollment. I looked at my ability to be organized and knew I could help other people become more organized, personally and professionally. With two small children, it's great to have the flexibility to set my own schedule. I love being a *professional organizer* so much, I doubt that I'll ever go back to teaching."

erty. Professional organizers usually are able to determine their own work hours.

Career Forecast

Growth of this career should be about average.

Monetary Rewards

Although professional organizers have been known to charge as much as $1,000 per hour, average fees range from $25 to $200 an hour. The yearly total earnings of a professional organizer depend entirely upon the number of wealthy clients. Professional organizers usually provide their own benefits.

Up the Ladder

Advancement is generally in the form of increased fame and a greater number of clients. More renowned organizers are able to charge higher fees for their services.

Related Jobs

- Executive assistant
- Human resource specialist
- Office manager

Gathering More Facts

National Association of Professional Organizers
P.O. Box 140647
Austin, TX 78714
Phone: (512) 206-0151
Internet: www.napo.net

Professional Organizers Web Ring
Internet: www.organizerswebring.com

68. *Small Animal Breeder*

DEFINITION

Small animal breeders raise and market small animals for fur buyers and laboratories.

TRANSFERABLE TEACHING SKILLS

- Scientific qualifications
- Organizational ability
- Decision-making skills

NECESSARY SKILLS

- Marketing
- Overseeing
- Administering

SUCCESS TIPS

- Have a love of animals
- Be structured
- Be organized

9 TO 5: HOW YOU WILL SPEND YOUR DAY

Small animal breeders fall into two major divisions: fur farmers and laboratory animal breeders. Fur farmers raise animals with high-quality fur, such as minks, squirrels, chinchillas, foxes, and rabbits. These animals are usually raised in outdoor cages and kept separate from each other to prevent them from damaging each other's pelts in fights. Animals must be fed and given water every day, and their cages kept clean. These tasks may be performed by hand or through automation. Fur farmers breed together animals with good pelts, to ensure successive generations of fine fur. When the pelts are in their prime, fur farmers must kill the animals, usually through injection or electrocution; skin them; and sell the furs.

Laboratory animals are used in medical laboratories and scientific experiments. These animals are typically rats, mice, guinea pigs, monkeys, chickens, cats, or dogs. Laboratory animal breeders care for their animals just as fur farmers do, except that they do not necessarily have to keep the animals separate. Laboratory animal breeders are concerned with keeping their animals healthy and breeding animals with specific traits, such as intelligence and curiosity.

Where You Will Spend Your Day

Small animal breeders have small operations and must work long hours every day of the week on their farms. Breeders with large operations may have more regular hours, because they typically have employees who take care of menial tasks.

Career Forecast

Because of heavy foreign competition, fur farmers are diminishing, but laboratory animal breeders are in constant demand.

Monetary Rewards

Earnings vary so widely that no ranges or averages may be estimated. Prices of animals and costs of raising animals are subject to extreme change from year to year. Self-employed breeders must provide their own benefits, but those employed by large organizations usually receive vacations and insurance.

Up the Ladder

Advancement is restricted to the growth of the breeder's farm. No other advancement opportunities exist for small animal breeders.

RELATED JOBS

- Animal trainer
- Farm manager
- Veterinarian

GATHERING MORE FACTS

National Association of Animal Breeders
P.O. Box 1033
Columbia, MO 65205-1033
Phone: (314) 445-4406
Internet: www.naab-oss.org

The American Rabbit Breeders Association, Inc.
P.O. Box 426
Bloomington, IL 61702
Phone: (309) 664-7500
Internet: www.arba.net

The Fur Commission U.S.A.
826 Orange Avenue
Coronado, CA 92118-2698
Phone: (619) 575-0139
Internet: www.furcommission.com

CHAPTER NINE

The Noble Public Servant

As a teacher, you have been a disciplinarian; you have laid down the rules and made sure that they were followed. You have enforced the law. Who says you can't be an FBI agent or a probation officer? Those are only a few of the job opportunities listed in this chapter. Many more options exist in the public service area, such as health inspector or public relations specialist. For people who want a little adventure in their lives, other choices could be flight attendant or animal control officer. This chapter describes career opportunities in which you provide a service that people need. The similarity between these jobs and teaching is that you are a disciplinarian as well as a good Samaritan.

69. FBI Agent

DEFINITION

FBI agents investigate violations of federal laws.

Transferable Teaching Skills

- Good communication
- Service orientation
- Judgment and decision making

Necessary Skills

- Must be a citizen of the United States and between the ages of 23 and 36
- Must be in excellent physical condition
- Must have stability, personal security, and a love of challenge

Success Tips

- Be mentally and emotionally strong enough to handle extreme stress

From Classroom to . . .

Tom Klese didn't know much about the Federal Bureau of Investigation. However, as he learned about the mission of the FBI, he became more interested. "I have always been athletic and like the opportunity to combine physical and mental challenges on the job. Being an *FBI agent* is very different from being a science teacher. I was never on call twenty-four hours a day, seven days a week, as a teacher. I never was called by the building principal in the middle of the night or required to work on the weekend.

"The screening process I went through included a four-hour written test, an oral interview, a polygraph examination, a urinalysis, a medical examination, and a complete background investigation. Every minute of the process was worth it because I really like being an agent and the variety of my assignments." Tom suggests that those interested in being a special agent should check out the FBI Web site to learn more about the application requirements.

- Have a strong sense of responsibility to the community
- Cultivate high values in integrity and honesty

9 TO 5: HOW YOU WILL SPEND YOUR DAY

FBI agents are responsible for investigating violations of federal laws and maintaining the security of our country. Agents typically work on their own, although danger or other factors may require partners. Agents have vast networks of contacts and a crime detection laboratory in Washington, D.C. Agents usually carry special identification and firearms while on duty.

WHERE YOU WILL SPEND YOUR DAY

FBI agents operate from any one or more of the offices or resident agency offices around the world. They are on call twenty-four hours a day, seven days a week. Assignments may be at any location, so they often must travel. Dangerous circumstances, because of the criminal element, are common.

CAREER FORECAST

Competition is extremely high because very few openings are available, even with the growth of federal crime. Individuals with college training in police science or other criminal justice courses will have the best opportunities in this field. The number of FBI agents needed may vary because the level of government spending can change from year to year.

MONETARY REWARDS

Salaries range from $34,000 to $100,000 per year, plus full benefits, overtime, and possible bonuses.

UP THE LADDER

Promotions are based upon agent performance, resulting in higher pay and better benefits.

RELATED JOBS

- Probation officer
- Correctional officer
- Security consultant

GATHERING MORE FACTS

The FBI Agents Association
P.O. Box 250
New Rochelle, NY 10801
Phone: (914) 235-7580
Internet: www.fbiaa.org

U.S. Department of Justice
The Federal Bureau of Investigation
J. Edgar Hoover Building
935 Pennsylvania Avenue, NW
Washington, DC 20535-0001
Phone: (202) 324-3000
Internet: www.fbi.gov/

This Internet site contains a wide variety of information about law enforcement jobs.
Internet: http://911hotjob.com

70. *Security Consultant and Technician*

DEFINITION

Security consultants and technicians design and create security plans and procedures to protect public and private property from damage and loss.

TRANSFERABLE TEACHING SKILLS

- Visioning
- Trouble-shooting
- Problem identification

NECESSARY SKILLS

- Alertness
- Honesty
- Compliance (ability to follow directions)

SUCCESS TIPS

- Stay in good health
- Be emotionally stable
- Be drug-free

9 TO 5: HOW YOU WILL SPEND YOUR DAY

For millennia, a common concern among those who accumulate material goods has been, and still is, the prevention of damage to, or loss of, those goods. The usual source of concern has been other people who covet those goods. However, people also exist who would just as soon destroy as steal material wealth. Because of this, quite sophisticated security plans and systems were created to help circumvent or capture these people. Security consultants organize security plans through the implementation of personnel and current technology, while security technicians serve as actual security personnel.

Security consultants begin their design stage by determining the employer's available budget for the new security plan. From this determination and an accompanying discussion with the employer on security goals, the security consultant can determine what equipment best suits both the security budget and security objectives. Although technology alone may be implemented, such as electronic eyes and ultrasonic motion detectors, security plans are usually fleshed out with security personnel as an extra safeguard.

Security technicians vary in title, from club bouncers to military security technicians to private security guards, but they all perform similar duties. They ensure that no intrusions escape the notice of electronic surveillance, and they monitor all electronic equipment.

WHERE YOU WILL SPEND YOUR DAY

Security consultants have offices they operate from, but they often work with a client at the client's business location to develop or improve a security plan. Security technicians, on the other hand, always work in a particular place, guarding a particular location. Consultants often determine their own hours, while security technicians are usually on rotating eight-hour shifts, including weekends and holidays.

CAREER FORECAST

The rise of crime rates, due to overall population increase, ensures definite growth in this career.

MONETARY REWARDS

Salaries for consultants range from $26,000 to more than $100,000 per year. Benefits include vacations, health insurance, and pension plans. Salaries for technicians range from $15,500 to $35,600 per year, with benefits similar to those of consultants.

UP THE LADDER

Security technicians generally receive periodic salary increases and increased rank. Seniority can provide them with a choice of work shifts. Security consultants with experience typically advance to either management positions or owning their own consulting firms.

RELATED JOBS

- Insurance agent
- Management analyst and consultant
- Real estate agent

GATHERING MORE FACTS

American Society for Industrial Security
1625 Prince Street
Alexandria, VA 22314
Phone: (703) 519-6200
Internet: http://asisonline.org

International Union of United Government Security
    Officers of America
7290 Samuel Drive, Suite 110
Denver, CO 80221
Phone: (800) 572-6103
Internet: www.ugsoa.com

International Union, Security Police and Fire Professionals
    of America (SPFPA)
Phone: (800) 228-7492
Internet: www.spfpa.org/

71. *Health and Regulatory Inspector*

DEFINITION

Health and regulatory inspectors enforce health and public
safety laws created by federal, state, and local governments.

TRANSFERABLE TEACHING SKILLS

- Critical thinking
- Monitoring
- Information gathering

Necessary Skills

- Must have a tenacious, patient eye for detail
- Must be able to communicate well with others
- Must be able to responsibly convey investigative conclusions to supervisor

Success Tips

- Be able to handle adversarial situations
- Be physically fit
- Be logical in helping others solve problems

9 to 5: How You Will Spend Your Day

There are so many areas to regulate that a variety of specializations are possible in this field, from food inspection to environmental health inspection to transportation inspection. All health and regulatory inspectors must undergo specialized training to learn the requirements that certain products and services must meet, as determined by federal, local, and state regulations. Health and regulatory inspectors ensure that consumers receive safe, healthful products and services. They also ensure that employees and employers operate their businesses according to safety and health standards. This is done through visits, interviews, and various types of spot checks.

Where You Will Spend Your Day

Health and regulatory inspectors must travel a lot to inspect the businesses in their region. Dangers include exposure to harmful substances or precarious situations as they seek to correct these problems. Often, work hours are irregular and very long, depending on the inspector's specialty and the frequency of regulation problems.

CAREER FORECAST

Most positions are already filled, but growth of job opportunities in this field is expected to increase as the public expects a safer environment and higher-quality products.

MONETARY REWARDS

Earnings range from $19,810 to $63,180 per year, plus benefits, overtime, and bonuses. Salaries and benefits for government inspectors and those in large corporations are usually higher and more generous.

UP THE LADDER

Advancement is dependent on satisfactory job performance. Advancement into supervisory positions is usually competitive and based on needs within the department or company.

RELATED JOBS

- FBI agent
- Probation officer
- Security technician

GATHERING MORE INFORMATION

Environmental Protection Agency
401 M Street, SW
Washington, DC 20460
Phone: (202) 260-2090
Internet: www.epa.gov

Occupational Safety and Health Administration
U.S. Department of Labor
Public Affairs Office, Room 3647
200 Constitution Avenue, NW
Washington, DC 20210

Phone: (202) 693-1999
Internet: www.osha.gov

Public Health Service
Department of Health and Human Services
200 Independence Avenue, SW
Washington, DC 20201
Phone: (202) 619-0257
Internet: http://phs.us.dhhs.gov/phs/

72. *Animal Control Officer*

DEFINITION

Animal control officers enforce animal control regulations, animal licensing, and leash laws.

TRANSFERABLE TEACHING SKILLS

- Reading comprehension
- Ability to write reports
- Interpersonal skills

NECESSARY SKILLS

- Knowledge of local animal control ordinances
- Knowledge of animal control enforcement procedures
- Supervision skills

SUCCESS TIPS

- Work well under stress
- Stay physically fit
- Have a knowledge of animal control

9 TO 5: HOW YOU WILL SPEND YOUR DAY

Animal control officers enforce the regulations and laws of animal control that protect the health and safety of humans and animals. They investigate and follow up reports of vicious dogs or stray animals. They also must investigate reports of animal mistreatment, sickness, and abandonment. Animal control officers enforce laws regarding rabies control, as well as licensing requirements for pet breeders. When officers discover violations, they write and issue warnings, citations, or summons. Animal control officers may be required to appear in court as witnesses in animal cruelty cases.

Officers may have to pursue and capture stray, unlicensed, or dangerous animals. They have to be skilled in using various tools to capture animals, including nets, catchall sticks, ropes, or traps. It is important that the officer use these tools in a humane manner. Once captured, the animals must be carefully transferred to cages for transport to a holding facility, such as the humane shelter. The officer might examine captured stray animals for license tags, ID microchips, and signs of illness or injury. If possible, the animal is returned to its owner.

Officers usually have an assigned area to patrol. This requires the officer to have a good knowledge of local streets or roadways. Animal control officers often assist law enforcement officers in resolving conflicts that involve animals. They may have to rescue animals in distress. While on patrol, officers talk with citizens about animal care, animal control laws, and licensing requirements. Education is becoming an important aspect of an animal control officer's duties. These officers hope to prevent animal control problems and violations.

Animal control officers may find themselves in stressful situations with citizens when enforcing regulations. They must maintain their composure and be firm and impartial when explaining regulations to the public. They must be tactful and courteous at all times. This job requires physical strength as well. Officers must be able to lift heavy animals and cages.

Where You Will Spend Your Day

Animal control officers spend much of their time patrolling their assigned area and responding to citizen reports. They usually have a truck or van with the equipment needed to capture, restrain, and transport animals. Some officers patrol on foot. Animal control officers might perform administrative duties at the humane shelter, such as collecting fees, assisting in communications, and completing kennel duties, which include overseeing animal care assistants working in the kennel operations area.

Officers typically work forty hours per week, but may have to be on call at night, on weekends, and through holidays to answer emergency calls.

Career Forecast

The pet population continues to grow; therefore, the need for animal control officers will increase. In addition, there tends to be a high turnover in the animal control area because of physical demands on animal control officers and their exposure to injury and disease as a result of dangerous or ill animals.

Monetary Rewards

Earnings for animal control officers vary, according to the size of the community and its commitment to animal control programs. On average, officers earn $21,200 per year. The greatest opportunities are in the upper-level trained positions in management and investigation. These workers can potentially earn from $50,000 to $85,000 in larger metropolitan areas.

Up the Ladder

Opportunities for advancement include supervisory or management positions. Smaller communities have limited opportunities for promotion because they often have only two or three animal control officers. Larger cities have more opportunities, such as field supervisor, shelter manager, or operations manager.

Related Jobs

- Zoologist
- Small animal breeder
- Pet sitter

Gathering More Facts

Humane Society of the United States
2100 L Street, NW
Washington, DC 20037
Phone: (202) 452-1100
Internet: www.hsus.org

Humane Society University
Humane Society of the United States
Training Incentives Section
2100 L Street, NW
Washington, DC 20037
Internet: www.humanesocietyu.org

National Animal Control Association
P.O. Box 480851
Kansas City, MO 64148
Phone: (913) 768-1319
Internet: www.nacanet.org

73. *Probation Officer*

Definition

Probation officers work with offenders who are given probation, which is the conditional suspension of a prison sentence after conviction.

TRANSFERABLE TEACHING SKILLS

- Social perceptiveness
- Information gathering
- Instructing

NECESSARY SKILLS

- Patience
- Good communication
- Ability to work with and motivate others

SUCCESS TIPS

- Be computer literate
- Be physically fit
- Be willing to be available twenty-four hours a day, seven days a week

9 TO 5: HOW YOU WILL SPEND YOUR DAY

Those offenders on probation must follow strict guidelines; failure to do so will result in imprisonment. Probation officers monitor these offenders and assist them in finding employment. Officers sometimes must make referrals to therapists and other specialists to aid offenders in their rehabilitation. Probation officers provide advice and guidance to offenders, as well as interview those around them to determine the extent of the offenders' rehabilitative needs.

WHERE YOU WILL SPEND YOUR DAY

Probation officers spend part of their time in government offices, processing paperwork on their assigned offenders. The rest of the time these officers visit probationers and their peers. Probation officers typically work forty hours a week, but they must be prepared to work at night or on weekends to accommodate probationers' work schedules.

CAREER FORECAST

Because of the rehabilitative interest in offenders, this career should grow at a faster than average rate.

MONETARY REWARDS

Salaries, depending on location and experience, range from $20,000 to $40,000 per year. Benefits vary widely, but usually include vacation time, medical insurance, and pension plans.

UP THE LADDER

Advancement occurs through passing civil service tests for regular promotions, salary increases, and increased supervisory responsibilities.

From Classroom to . . .

Andrew Parker has been a *juvenile probation officer* for more than fifteen years. "I became interested in the probation career while teaching high school. Several students who came through my classes got into trouble and required instruction at the juvenile detention center. Because I thought these kids deserved the chance to finish their classes, I agreed to go to the detention facility and teach them. The probation officer supervising the students told me about his job. I applied for a vacancy in the probation department because I wanted to help the kids get back on the right track. It is disappointing to have some of the kids get in more trouble and end up doing time at a detention facility. On the other hand, it's very satisfying to see many of my clients succeed in completing their probation and graduate from high school. Some go on to college and have successful careers in their adult lives."

RELATED JOBS

- Park ranger
- Security technician
- FBI agent

GATHERING MORE FACTS

American Federation of State, County, and Municipal
    Employees
1625 L Street, NW
Washington, DC 20036
Phone: (202) 429-1000
Internet: www.afscme.org

National Council on Crime and Delinquency
1970 Broadway, Suite 500
Oakland, CA 94612
Telephone: (510) 208-0500
Internet: www.nccd-crc.org

The American Correctional Association
4380 Forbes Boulevard
Lanham, MD 20706-5646
Phone: (800) 222-5646
Internet: www.corrections.com

74. *Public Relations Specialist*

DEFINITION

Public relations specialists implement strategies to create a
favorable public image for individuals or organizations.

TRANSFERABLE TEACHING SKILLS

- Information organization
- Service orientation
- Critical thinking

NECESSARY SKILLS

- Ability to understand how to achieve successful business performance
- Strong writing and speaking skills
- Excellent interpersonal skills

SUCCESS TIPS

- Have strong leadership skills
- Be very organized
- Have excellent integrity

9 TO 5: HOW YOU WILL SPEND YOUR DAY

Public relations specialists perform a variety of tasks: writing reports, speeches, and news releases; editing communications; contacting media on behalf of the employer; handling special events; making appearances before groups; and supervising the advertising of the employer's name and reputation. A public relations specialist must confer with management staff to ensure that the employer or representatives of the employing company conduct themselves in a way that earns the confidence of the public. Public relations specialists must be aware of any and all meetings, news releases, and innovations.

WHERE YOU WILL SPEND YOUR DAY

Public relations specialists spend part of their time in an office with some secretarial help; at all times they are expected to be dressed tastefully and conservatively. Conventional office hours are rare, because public relations specialists must attend events at night, on weekends, and whenever they occur.

CAREER FORECAST

Competition for public relations specialists will be high, but those with education and experience will have the best opportunities for the limited positions.

Monetary Rewards

Salaries range from $15,000 to $150,000 a year, with an average of $34,500 per year. Benefits will vary, depending on location, experience, and the wealth of the employing company.

Up the Ladder

Advancement is in the form of increased responsibilities, salary, and benefits; some may choose to work with a different company that offers better pay and benefits.

Related Jobs

- Fundraiser
- Advertising/marketing consultant
- Police officer involved in community relations

Gathering More Facts

International Association of Business Communicators
One Halladie Plaza, Suite 600
San Francisco, CA 94102
Phone: (800) 776-4222
Internet: www.iabc.com

PR Reporter
PR Publishing Company Inc.
P.O. Box 600
Exeter, NH 03833
Phone: (603) 778-0514
Internet: www.prpublishing.com

Public Relations Society of America
Career Information
33 Irving Place
New York, NY 10003
Phone: (212) 995-2230
Internet: www.prsa.org

75. *Religious Vocation*

DEFINITION

Clergy members are the spiritual leaders and advisers within any of the religious faiths in our country.

TRANSFERABLE TEACHING SKILLS

- Active listening
- Time management
- Social perceptiveness

NECESSARY SKILLS

- Strong interpersonal skills
- Sympathetic nature and patience under stress
- Strong leadership skills

SUCCESS TIPS

- Be committed to be available twenty-four hours a day
- Be involved in the community
- Develop extraordinary coping skills

9 TO 5: HOW YOU WILL SPEND YOUR DAY

Clergy members are the leaders and organizers of their community's religious activities. They lead religious services, often by delivering sermons. They conduct weddings and funeral services. Clergy often serve as counselors to members of their religious faith. Clergy members perform various other tasks, depending upon their religion; for example, Roman Catholic priests hear confessions.

Clergy members also perform secular or nonreligious tasks, particularly in community improvement. They might participate in interfaith services to span the gap between religious faiths or organize community activities that are aimed at bettering the community.

From Classroom to . . .

Today Tom Clegg is a *Catholic priest*. However, he has had many different careers while struggling with the idea that maybe he was called to serve God. After high school, Tom began to study at the seminary but then dropped out to enter the insurance business. A short time later, he returned to the seminary and then decided to go back to college for an education degree. "I started teaching eighth grade at a Catholic grade school. While I was teaching, I decided to coach a Little League team. When one of my little league players suddenly died, I felt the call to return to the seminary. I still have many opportunities to use my teaching skills with parishioners. It's tremendously satisfying to share God with others, to help them deepen their faith, and to counsel and comfort parishioners in times of need."

WHERE YOU WILL SPEND YOUR DAY

Clergy members can work almost anywhere, from a majestic cathedral to a foreign jungle to a local ghetto. A religious vocation is a twenty-four-hour a day, seven-day a week job, and members of the clergy must be prepared to be called upon by their church members at any time.

CAREER FORECAST

Outlook for this career depends upon the religious faith. The need for Protestant ministers has slowed considerably. Opportunities within other faiths are growing.

MONETARY REWARDS

Salaries depend entirely upon the congregation's size, location, and religious faith. Benefits supplement the salary and somewhat offset lower salaries.

Up the Ladder

Depending on the religious faith, advancement, if it exists, is in the form of increased administrative responsibilities in a larger church or parish.

Related Jobs

- Counselor
- Social worker
- College student personnel worker

Gathering More Facts

Association of Theological Schools in the United States
and Canada
10 Summit Park Drive
Pittsburgh, PA 15275-1103
Phone: (412) 788-6505
Internet: http://ats.edu

Center for Applied Research in the Apostolate (CARA)
Georgetown University
Washington, DC 20057
Phone: (202) 687-8080

National Council of the Churches of Christ in the U.S.A.
475 Riverside Drive, Room 880
New York, NY 10115-0050
Phone: (212) 870-2141

76. *Flight Attendant*

Definition

Flight attendants are responsible for the safety and comfort of airline passengers.

Transferable Teaching Skills

- Service orientation
- Excellent interpersonal skills
- Problem identification

Necessary Skills

- Intelligence, poise, and resourcefulness in emergencies
- A congenial temperament
- Excellent health

Success Tips

- Be willing to complete the training program (four to seven weeks)
- Be able to relocate
- College courses in psychology, education, or both are helpful

9 to 5: How You Will Spend Your Day

Flight attendants' duties begin an hour before takeoff, when they help check all equipment for flight readiness. Flight attendants also inspect the galley to be sure it is stocked and secured. Flight attendants are an important part of the security checks necessary for a safe flight. They welcome passengers and check their tickets. They aid passengers whenever necessary in storing luggage. Flight attendants must demonstrate the use of safety equipment and provide passengers with safety information. During the flight, attendants sometimes serve food and drinks and distribute reading materials.

Where You Will Spend Your Day

Flight attendants usually have a home-based city from which they operate. Work may be at any time of the day, any time of the year, and particularly during holidays. Although they travel quite a bit, their free time at destinations is limited by tight flight schedules.

Career Forecast

Career opportunities within the airline industry are closely tied to the economy and the need or desire for consumer travel. Individuals with experience in dealing with the public will have better opportunities.

Monetary Rewards

Earnings range from $12,800 to $40,000 a year, with full benefits and overtime. Senior flight attendants can earn as much as $50,000 per year. Airlines do provide additional benefits, including free fares on their own carriers for their employees and employees' immediate families and discounted fares on other carriers.

Up the Ladder

Advancement involves greater responsibilities on flights, with higher pay, seniority, and benefits. Some attendants move into supervisory positions or become recruiters or instructors for their airline.

Related Jobs

- Social worker
- Travel agent
- Adventure travel specialist

Gathering More Facts

Air Transport Association of America
1302 Pennsylvania Avenue, NW, Suite 1100
Washington, DC 20004-1707
Phone: (202) 626-4000
Internet: www.air-transport.org/

AirlineCareer.com
Internet: www.airlinecareer.com

Association of Flight Attendants
1275 K Street, NW, Suite 500
Washington, DC 20005-4090
Phone: (202) 712-9799
Internet: www.afanet.org

77. *Social Worker*

DEFINITION

Social workers counsel people with personal problems, such as poverty, sickness, and family trouble.

TRANSFERABLE TEACHING SKILLS

- Monitoring
- Social perceptiveness
- Critical thinking

NECESSARY SKILLS

- Maturity, sensitivity, and patience
- Strong communication
- Strong interpersonal skills

SUCCESS TIPS

- Be decisive
- Be an excellent problem solver
- Be sympathetic and tolerant

9 TO 5: HOW YOU WILL SPEND YOUR DAY

Social workers provide a number of services, from finding foster homes for children to aiding disaster victims. Some social workers work in the school systems, where they counsel students with family and school problems. Some work in hospitals to counsel patients with disabilities and terminal illnesses. Others take one of three approaches to social work: casework, group work, or community organization work. Caseworkers counsel individuals and families, while group social workers counsel and aid groups of people with similar problems. Community organization workers develop programs that address social problems within their district.

WHERE YOU WILL SPEND YOUR DAY

Social workers can be found in nearly every city, suburb, or rural area. Schools, hospitals, offices, and jails are just some of the places that need social workers. They typically work thirty-five to forty hours per week, although they may be called at any time for emergencies.

CAREER FORECAST

The outlook is good for this growing field, but opportunities are best for those individuals with graduate degrees or experience.

From Classroom to . . .

Jolene Addington understands the importance of communication as a *caseworker for child protective services*. "I have to be able to talk to children as well as adults, speak effectively in a courtroom, and use proper terminology with my colleagues and supervisor. What I say can have a tremendous impact on a family. That responsibility can be stressful for any caseworker. As an elementary teacher, I frequently talked to the parents of my students about problems or academic concerns. Those conferences rarely carried the responsibility and impact of the conferences I have as a caseworker. The most rewarding aspect of my job is helping families overcome problems and reunify."

MONETARY REWARDS

Salaries range from $20,000 a year to more than $45,000. Benefits are usually good, but the best-paying jobs are federal administrative positions.

UP THE LADDER

Advancement consists of administrative or teaching positions, attainable through college degrees and social work experience.

RELATED JOBS

- Clergy
- Counselor
- Probation officer

GATHERING MORE FACTS

American Association for Marriage and Family Therapy
1133 15th Street, NW, Suite 300
Washington, DC 20005-2710
Phone: (202) 452-0109
Internet: www.aamft.org

American Federation of State, County, and Municipal
    Employees
1625 L Street, NW
Washington, DC 20036
Phone: (202) 429-1000
Internet: www.afscme.org

National Association of Social Workers
750 First St. NE, Suite 700
Washington, DC 20002-4241
Phone: (202) 408-8600
Internet: www.naswdc.org

78. *Zoo and Aquarium Curator*

DEFINITION

Zoo and aquarium curators are directly responsible for the care of their employing institutions' animals.

TRANSFERABLE TEACHING SKILLS

- Overseeing
- Processing
- Supervising

NECESSARY SKILLS

- Interpersonal skills
- Good communication
- Compassion

SUCCESS TIPS

- Have a knowledge of animals
- Be organized and efficient when administering
- Be a problem solver

9 TO 5: HOW YOU WILL SPEND YOUR DAY

In the past, curators simply were responsible for the well-being of the zoo's or aquarium's animals, but the growth of these institutions has expanded the duties and the degrees of curatorship. General curators are at the top of the curator ladder. General curators serve as advisers to their institutions' directors, whom they help to coordinate and create activities and long-term plans. General curators create policies in their supervision of the institution's animal collection and animal management staff. Other curators implement these policies.

Animal curators oversee the operations and animal husbandry, such as daily care, nutrition, and veterinary health.

Curators develop exhibits, visitor services, and educational programs. They must also keep an inventory of the animals in their charge. They make recommendations based on these inventories and offer personal judgments on the acquisition and disposition of animals. Curators prepare budgets for directorial approval and develop reports to keep their supervisors informed. Curators may also serve as instructional representatives to the public.

WHERE YOU WILL SPEND YOUR DAY

Curators typically spend their time in pleasant, on-site offices, performing administrative duties. Interaction with animals is restricted to emergencies. Work hours are usually long and include weekends and holidays. Travel may sometimes be necessary to attend conferences or visit other zoos.

CAREER FORECAST

Because of the lack of new zoos and aquariums, this field will experience a much slower than average growth rate in job opportunities.

MONETARY REWARDS

Salaries, depending on factors such as institution size and location, range from $20,000 to $79,000 per year, with an average of $40,000 per year. Benefits include health insurance, vacations, and retirement plans; corporate institutions may offer profit sharing.

UP THE LADDER

Curators may advance to executive positions, such as general curator or director, or to a similar position in a larger, better-paying institution. Graduate education and experience typically lead to advancement.

Related Jobs

- Historian
- Information specialist
- Records manager

Gathering More Facts

American Association of Zoo Keepers, Inc
Topeka Zoological Park
635 Southwest Gage Boulevard
Topeka, KS 66606-2066
Phone: (785) 273-1980
Internet: www.aazk.org

American Zoo and Conservation Center
79700-D Old Georgetown Road
Bethesda, MD 20814-2493
Internet: www.aza.org

Conservation Breeding Specialist Group
12101 Johnny Cake Ridge Road
Apple Valley, MN 55124-8151
Phone: (952) 997-9800
Internet: www.cbsg.org

79. *Urban Planner*

Definition

Urban planners develop short- and long-term plans for land usage for community development and economic growth.

Transferable Teaching Skills

- Developing
- Coordinating
- Budgeting

Necessary Skills

- Good communication
- Organizational ability
- Computer literacy

Success Tips

- Know and enforce the zoning and building codes
- Organize groups of people
- Anticipate needs

9 to 5: How You Will Spend Your Day

Urban planners endorse the best possible use of community land for recreational, commercial, and residential benefits. Planners are also involved in other activities, including making decisions on resource developments and alternative transportation plans. They evaluate the effects that certain changes like air pollution might have on a community. Planners evaluate a proposed facility's ability to compensate for demands that will be placed upon it by consistent population growth. They also stay up-to-date on local building and zoning codes and environmental regulations.

Prior to preparing plans for community development, planners consider current use of land for various reasons. These considerations include recreational and cultural sites, water and sewer lines, streets, highways, schools, and libraries. Planners also provide information on the complex demographics of the community, including industry, economic patterns, and employment.

Planners often consult with land developers or public officials. Planners may act as mediators to resolve community disputes and may present solutions to the problem. In small organizations, planners are responsible for various aspects of community planning. In larger organizations, planners typically concentrate on one specific area of expertise, ranging from housing to transportation or economic development.

Where You Will Spend Your Day

Besides working in an office, urban planners are often on the road, visiting locations of proposed building sites and then making return visits to oversee that all zoning and building codes are followed. Planners also inspect city buildings to make sure these are up-to-date on all codes. Back in the office, reports must be generated for other officials before projects can be started.

Career Forecast

The outlook for urban planners is anticipated to have a growth spurt until around 2008. This is due to more state and local agencies providing additional public services for residents. Many urban planners work for local governments or housing, transportation, or environmental protection agencies.

Monetary Rewards

Earnings for urban planners range from $32,920 to $56,150 a year. Those planners with more experience may earn as much as $80,000 per year.

Up the Ladder

Advancement for most planners comes with additional education and training. Some may move to a specialized area of urban planning or to a larger jurisdiction, which will have additional responsibilities.

Related Jobs

- City manager
- Director of community development
- Landscape architect

Gathering More Facts

American Planning Association
Education Division
122 South Michigan Avenue, Suite 1600
Chicago, IL 60603
Phone: (312) 431-9100
Internet: www.planning.org

Congress for the New Urbanism
5 Third Street, Suite 725
San Francisco, CA 94103
Phone: (415) 495-2255
Internet: www.cnu.org

Council of Planning Librarians
101 North Wacker Drive, Suite CM-190
Chicago, IL 60606
Phone (312) 409-3349
Internet: www.west.asu.edu/mmyers/cpl

80. *Postal Service Worker*

Definition

Postal service workers collect, sort, and deliver mail, such as letters, bills, advertisements, and packages.

Transferable Teaching Skills

- Speaking ability
- Talent for being organized
- Interpersonal skills

Necessary Skills

- Good memory
- Ability to read quickly and accurately
- Team player

Success Tips

- Handle the pressure of deadlines
- Be courteous
- Be physically fit

9 to 5: How You Will Spend Your Day

The U.S. Postal Service employs nearly one million people. About two-thirds of these employees are postal clerks and mail carriers. Postal clerks may work directly with customers, selling them stamps, stationary, envelopes, and boxes. Clerks collect mail from customers who need to insure, register, or certify mail or packages. They also answer customer questions. Other postal clerks are responsible for sorting mail for delivery. They operate the sorting machines known as optical character readers. In smaller post offices, clerks may sort the mail by hand.

After clerks sort the mail, the mail carriers begin the process of delivery. Carriers may complete their route on foot, by vehicle, or both. Most rural carriers use their own vehicle. Mail carriers also get customer signatures for insured, registered, or certified mail and collect fees for COD or postage-due mail. After their route is complete, carriers return to the post office. They turn in collected mail, money, and receipts.

Where You Will Spend Your Day

Postal clerks work in the clean, well-lit customer service area. Sorting clerks work in areas with machines, conveyors, and chutes. Their work is physically demanding and routine, even monotonous. Large post offices sort mail twenty-four hours a day, seven days a week.

Mail carriers may begin work very early in the morning and finish by early afternoon. They spend most of their time outside in all kinds of weather. Motor routes can be very hazardous, especially during the winter months. Carriers might have to work overtime during the peak delivery times, such as just before holidays.

CAREER FORECAST

There is much competition for postal service jobs. Limited job opportunities exist, even though the postal service looks to improve customer service with more window clerks. Technological advances in machinery will cause a decreased need for sorting clerks.

MONETARY REWARDS

The average annual salary for mail carriers is $34,800. Postal service clerks earn an average of $35,100 per year. Benefits include health and life insurance, vacation and sick leave, and pension plans. Most postal service workers are members of either the American Postal Workers Union or the National Association of Letter Carriers.

UP THE LADDER

Postal clerks generally advance to more preferred assignments, which may include working the day shift or some type of supervisory position. Postal carriers may bid on preferred routes, carrier technician positions, or a supervisory position.

RELATED JOBS

- Customer service representative
- Equipment operator
- Messenger

GATHERING MORE FACTS

American Postal Workers Union
1300 L Street, NW
Washington, DC 20005
Phone: (202) 842-4200 or (202) 842-8500
Internet: www.apwu.org

National Association of Letter Carriers
100 Indiana Avenue, NW
Washington, DC 20001-2144
Phone: (202) 393-4695
Internet: www.nalc.org

U.S. Postal Service
Phone: (800) 275-8777
Internet: www.usps.com
   OR
contact your local post office

Publish or Perish

Applying for any of the jobs in this chapter indicates that you enjoy the written word. Most teachers are used to being surrounded by printed material. In fact, some teachers even echo John Adams's sentiment, "I cannot live without books." If you have no problem spending eight or more hours daily reading, creating, or correcting the printed word, you would enjoy a career move into the publishing world.

Excitement and a wide variety of opportunities abound in the publishing field. Keep in mind that it takes many different people to get a book or other printed materials from the author's hands to the reader. Some of these people are the editors, proofreaders, and literary agents. In this chapter you will read about these careers and many other opportunities in publishing.

Book publishing companies come in all sizes. You could find employment in a large company that employs thousands of people or a smaller company that employs only a few people. Or you might get a publishing job at a newspaper, magazine, or even online.

If you can handle the stress of deadlines, enjoy being part of a team, and have a talent for making the printed

word come alive to others, a job in publishing could be right
for you.

81. Book Editor

DEFINITION

Editors read and evaluate manuscripts for errors and details.

TRANSFERABLE TEACHING SKILLS

- Quickness in spotting errors
- Good command of the English language
- Love of reading

NECESSARY SKILLS

- Computer literacy
- Being motivated
- Punctuality

SUCCESS TIPS

- Be able to select good material that would appeal to others
- Have a good eye for detail
- Be able to handle pressure

9 TO 5: HOW YOU WILL SPEND YOUR DAY

The editor's primary responsibility is to evaluate all manuscripts. Editorial positions range from executive directors to
editors who evaluate only final copies for grammatical errors.
Usually, no single editor handles every aspect of manuscript
evaluation, but every editor is expected to know all the
requirements of the editorial positions. Editors may solicit
manuscripts from authors and literary agents, particularly if

the manuscripts desired are technical, professional, or sequels to successful works.

WHERE YOU WILL SPEND YOUR DAY

Book editors are usually limited in their choice of environment, which is typically an office in the main administrative buildings of the publishing company. At times, evaluative work may be completed at home or in some other relaxing environment, but most work, including phone solicitation of manuscripts, is done in an office.

CAREER FORECAST

Jobs for online and freelance editors will increase rapidly for the next several years. However, keep in mind that the turn-over rate for most editors is quite high.

From Classroom to . . .

"When I decided to go into book publishing after being a teacher, it was like learning a whole new language. It took months to learn all the publishing terms and to understand the complex process of producing a book: acquiring, editing, design, manufacturing, and promotion. However, my background as an English teacher helped me tremendously because I came into the job with the editing skills necessary and a fairly good eye for evaluating each author's writing ability, chapter development, and so on. After dealing with kids all those years in the classroom, I was a natural at handling temperamental authors! I can't imagine a more interesting career than publishing!"

—SUSAN, *book editor*

Monetary Rewards

Salaries range from $25,000 for editorial assistants to $88,700 for supervisory editors. Benefits are average.

Up the Ladder

Advancement is in one of two forms—freelance publishing or the acquisition of administrative duties in the same firm or in another firm. Salaries and benefits, of course, increase with advancement, along with job security.

Related Jobs

- Advertising
- Reporter
- Proofreader

Gathering More Facts

Association of American Publishers
71 Fifth Avenue
New York, NY 10003-3004
Phone: (212) 255-0200
Internet: www.publishers.org

Florida Publishers Association (Independent Publishers)
P.O. Box 430
Highland City, FL 33846-0430
Phone: (941) 647-5951
Internet: www.flbookpub.org

Small Publishers Association of North America
P.O. Box 1306
425 Cedar Street
Buena Vista, CO 81211
Phone: (719) 3954790
Internet: www.spannet.org

82. *Columnist*

DEFINITION

A columnist is a writer who produces columns for magazines, newspapers, or other periodicals.

TRANSFERABLE TEACHING SKILLS

- Ability to clearly express ideas
- Command of the English language
- Ability to meet deadlines

NECESSARY SKILLS

- Precision
- Thoroughness
- Persistence

SUCCESS TIPS

- Be computer literate
- Enjoy working outside an office
- Be able to clearly and creatively express your opinions

9 TO 5: HOW YOU WILL SPEND YOUR DAY

Columnists write columns on a regular basis, which could be daily, weekly, monthly, or quarterly. Columnists take news stories and elaborate on the facts of the story, based on personal experiences and opinion. The column usually contains a catchy beginning, a concise center, and an aggressive, sharp finale.

Most columnists are able to select their own topics to write about. Topics are found in newspapers, television, magazines, radio, and, most recently, the Internet. This is usually how columnists stay aware of current events. They also investigate the topic in order to substantiate their claims with facts, and finally, columnists write their articles. Once a column is written, one or more editors will proofread the article for errors and content.

WHERE YOU WILL SPEND YOUR DAY

Columnists work indoors most of the time. However, occasional research and interviews are conducted outside of the office.

CAREER FORECAST

The projected outlook for columnist positions with magazines is expected to increase, but the number of jobs for newspapers is expected to decrease. For smaller newspapers, columnists will sometimes be expected to assume reporting responsibilities as well. Overall, job opportunities for columnists are growing about as fast as the average.

MONETARY REWARDS

As with reporters, columnists earn a varying salary, depending on their experience, the newspaper size, whether they've signed a union contract, and their geographical location. According to the Dow Jones Newspaper Fund, columnists earn a starting salary of approximately $20,000. Experienced columnists can earn $60,000 or more annually.

UP THE LADDER

Syndication is the key to exposure and career advancement for columnists. Advancement can also be gained by columnists assuming other positions, such as editor, editorial writer, page editor, or foreign correspondent.

RELATED JOBS

- Proofreader
- Public relations specialist
- Advertising

From Classroom to . . .

"As a junior high school language arts teacher, I've always enjoyed both reading and writing. When I saw an ad in our local newspaper for an education columnist, I decided to apply. I love my new career. In fact, I've always had a love affair with words. I enjoy playing with words. However, I do have constant deadlines and there is pressure to meet the deadlines. Another challenge of writing a column is the word restriction. My story must fit into the space that is allotted.

"Along with having to research current educational issues, I find people to interview for each specific story to give my column a personal feel. My experiences in education are a definite advantage because I understand what educators are telling me when I interview them. I love getting the educational news out to our community, and I feel that the career move to become a full-time newspaper columnist is very exciting. I might even start trying to freelance some educational issue columns to magazines. I love the freedom to work from the office, take my laptop on site, or even work from my home."

—STEPHANIE PEARMAN, *educational columnist*

GATHERING MORE FACTS

American Society of Journalists and Authors
1501 Broadway, Suite 302
New York, NY 10036
Phone: (212) 997-0947
Internet: www.asja.org

National Association of Broadcasters
1771 N Street, NW
Washington, DC 20036
Phone: (202) 429-5300
Internet: www.nab.org

Society of Journalists
3909 North Meridian Street
Indianapolis, IN 46208
Phone: (317) 927-8000
Internet: www.spj.org

83. *Technical Writer and Editor*

DEFINITION

A writer who specializes in technical and scientific reports and manuals.

TRANSFERABLE TEACHING SKILLS

- Critical thinking
- Information gathering
- Meeting deadlines

NECESSARY SKILLS

- Self-motivation
- Scientific and technical aptitude
- Ability to handle pressure and be a team player

SUCCESS TIPS

- Be a team player
- Have knowledge of a specialized field (business, law, or engineering)
- Be able to work with publishing software

9 TO 5: HOW YOU WILL SPEND YOUR DAY

Technical writers and editors prepare manuals, technical reports, specifications, and proposals, all of which may be any length. Work begins with an assignment to a document, often as part of a team of technical advisers, writers, and editors, depending upon the size of the document and of the company. Together, these people plan, research, compose, and edit the document.

Sometimes, a technical writer or editor specializes in a specific medium. Scriptwriters create film scripts. Technical marketing writers prepare promotional works for technological products. A recent field is online writing and editing.

WHERE YOU WILL SPEND YOUR DAY

Technical writers and editors usually work in quiet, well-lit offices with an abundance of computer technology. Homes are sometimes converted into similar offices. Technical writers mostly work 40 hours per week, but sometimes must work 50 to 60 hours to meet project deadlines.

CAREER FORECAST

These competitive fields will grow slightly, but more people try to enter them than there are available openings.

MONETARY REWARDS

Salaries range from $28,600 to $72,000 a year, with the average being $47,440 a year. Most companies offer full benefits as part of their salary package.

UP THE LADDER

Advancement is in the form of greater administrative responsibility, freelancing opportunities, or choice of projects. All of these opportunities include higher salaries and fuller benefits.

RELATED JOBS

- Reporter
- News analyst
- Public relations specialist

GATHERING MORE FACTS

Association for Educational Communications and
Technology
1800 North Stonelake Drive, Suite 2
Bloomington, IN 47404
Phone: (812) 335-7675
Internet: www.aect.org

Information Technology Communicators Association (ITCA)
8343B Greensboro Drive
McLean, VA 22102
Phone: (703) 757-0520
Internet: www.itcomm.org

Society for Technical Communication
901 North Stuart Street, Suite 904
Arlington, VA 22203
Phone: (703) 522-4114
E-mail: stc@stc-va.org
Internet: www.stc.org

84. Grant Coordinator and Writer

DEFINITION

Someone who writes, oversees, or both, the preparation and
implementation of grants.

TRANSFERABLE TEACHING SKILLS

* Comprehension of written material
* Ability to meet deadlines
* Computer skills

NECESSARY SKILLS

* Precision
* Problem-solving ability
* Negotiation

Success Tips

- Be able to identify criteria
- Possess good organizational skills
- Express needs clearly

9 to 5: How You Will Spend Your Day

Grant coordinators oversee every aspect of an organization's application for funds, while grant writers write the actual applications for funds. Both coordinators and writers must first determine the amount of funds needed and in what areas these are needed. Then they prepare proposals to potential funders. These proposals must map out specifically how grant funds would be utilized. Executives within the organization must approve the grant proposals.

Once grants are actually obtained, grant coordinators must ensure that the funds are spent exactly according to the stipulations and expectations of funding organization. Grant coordinators are basically project managers.

Where You Will Spend Your Day

Grant coordinators and writers usually work during regular office hours in comfortable offices. Overtime work, both nights and weekends, may be required to meet deadlines. Travel is possible for meetings with potential funding organizations, but the majority of the work is done in an office environment.

Career Forecast

Because successful grant coordinators always find work, this field is dwindling, except for work in agencies only now realizing the benefits of using grant coordinators and writers.

Monetary Rewards

Earnings range from $18,000 to $69,000 a year, with an average of $41,300 a year. Full benefits are usually available.

From Classroom to ...

"Being a *grant writer* is a very challenging job," says Scott Stapleton. "I've been a freelance grant writer for over seven years. I got my start by writing a technology proposal for the elementary school I taught for. The feelings of excitement and pride when that proposal was accepted were indescribable. After overseeing the implementation of that proposal, I decided to volunteer to write a grant proposal for the community literacy organization. My freelance writing career grew out of this and several more volunteer projects for nonprofit groups. While it is a challenging career, I find it very satisfying to help worthwhile organizations in my area expand and help more people."

Up the Ladder

Advancement for grant coordinators usually involves moving to larger organizations. Grant writers may sometimes advance to be grant coordinators.

Related Jobs

- Fundraiser
- Lobbyist
- Technical writer

Gathering More Facts

American Association of Fund-Raising Counsels
10293 North Meridian Street, Suite 175
Indianapolis, IN 46290
Phone: (317) 816-1613 or (800) 462-2372
Internet: www.aafrc.org

Association of Fundraising Professionals
1101 King Street, Suite 700
Alexandria, VA 22314-2967

Phone: (703) 684-0410
Internet: www.nsfre.org

The Grantsmanship Center (TGCI)
1125 West Sixth Street, Fifth Floor
P.O. Box 17220
Los Angeles, CA 90017
Phone: (213) 482-9860
Internet: www.tgci.com

85. Indexer

DEFINITION

Indexers create indexes, or organized lists, to help others find information in a text or collection of works.

TRANSFERABLE TEACHING SKILLS

- Following rules
- Information organization
- Computer knowledge

NECESSARY SKILLS

- Alphabetization
- Consistency
- Organization

SUCCESS TIPS

- Cultivate an eye for detail
- Be able to work independently
- Handle the pressure of deadlines calmly

9 TO 5: HOW YOU WILL SPEND YOUR DAY

Several types of indexes exist. Most common is the back-of-book index contained in the back of most single-volume, nonfiction works. A multi-volume index, located in a separate volume or in the back of a series of volumes, is similar to the back-of-book index. Periodical indexes are published for magazines and newspapers as separate volumes; these serve as guides to many issues for researchers. An online index is a large database that serves as a translation thesaurus for an Internet search engine. Not all terms given the search engine by users may be found as they are, so synonyms must be provided by the online index. Nearly all indexes are listed alphabetically, although some may be chronological or numerical.

An indexer must read and comprehend a text before beginning the tracing process. Key terms and concepts are marked. After this process, headings, subheadings, and page references are compiled. Then, the index is edited. The index's organization is polished, trivial references are deleted, and subheadings are created for long entries. Usually, indexers create indexes by key words and concepts to cover specific terminology and synonyms simultaneously.

WHERE YOU WILL SPEND YOUR DAY

Full-time indexers work in pleasant offices, while freelance indexers work at home or at employers' offices. Many indexers work 40-hour weeks, although newspaper indexers regularly have much longer weeks. Freelance indexers have no definite hours, as these depend entirely upon project deadlines.

CAREER FORECAST

As the information industry rapidly grows, this field will also grow to provide easy searching to the public.

MONETARY REWARDS

Salaries for full-time indexers range from $20,000 to $30,000 a year, while freelancers may earn from $20,000 to $70,000 a year. Freelancers must provide their own benefits, while full-time indexers have average benefits—health insurance, vacation time, and a retirement plan.

Up the Ladder

Full-time indexers with experience may obtain seniority or even supervisory positions in their department. Freelancers are able to charge higher rates once they gain experience.

Related Jobs

- Database specialists
- Information services
- Research assistant

Gathering More Facts

American Society of Indexers
10200 West 44th Avenue, Suite 304
Wheat Ridge, CO 80033
Phone: (303) 463-2887
Internet: www.asindexing.org

American Society of Journalists and Authors
1501 Broadway, Suite 302
New York, NY 10036
Phone: (212) 997-0947
Internet: www.asja.org

Editorial Freelancers Association
71 West 23rd Street, Suite 1910
New York, NY 10010
Phone: (212) 929-5400
Internet: www.the-efa.org

86. *Periodical Editor*

DEFINITION

A periodical editor edits periodical publications.

TRANSFERABLE TEACHING SKILLS

- A critical eye
- Command of the English language
- Strong communication skills

NECESSARY SKILLS

- Excellent writing skills
- Experience in journalism
- Ability to make judgments

SUCCESS TIPS

- Have a wide range of knowledge
- Have strong positive reinforcement and motivational skills
- Be willing to explore internship opportunities to gain practical experience

9 TO 5: HOW YOU WILL SPEND YOUR DAY

A periodical editor is directly responsible for the format of the publication, both in design and in content. A periodical editor oversees every aspect of the publication's preparation in order to ensure that the periodical is competitive in its subject matter. Periodical editors must constantly supervise writers to ensure that publication deadlines are met. These editors often write editorials for their own publications; they have virtually unlimited power to edit submissions, hire writers, and rewrite articles.

WHERE YOU WILL SPEND YOUR DAY

Most of the periodical editor's work is completed in an office environment, although some work may require travel or may require work to be taken home. Work hours can be average (35 to 40 per week), but periodical editors often must work into the night and on weekends to meet publication deadlines.

CAREER FORECAST

As more special interest magazines are launched, many editors will be needed who have knowledge of, or experience in, those specialty areas.

MONETARY REWARDS

Earnings typically range from $11,000 to $68,000, with an average of $36,000 per year. Additional benefits vary, depending upon the success of the periodical.

UP THE LADDER

Advancement is usually through employment with a more successful periodical.

RELATED JOBS

- Proofreader
- Reporter
- Public relations

GATHERING MORE FACTS

American Society of Journalists and Authors
1501 Broadway, Suite 302
New York, NY 10036
Phone: (212) 997-0947
Internet: www.asja.org

American Society of Magazine Editors
919 Third Avenue, 22nd Floor
New York, NY 10022
Phone: (212) 872-3700
Internet: www.asme.magazine.org

The Newspaper Guild
501 Third Street, NW, Suite 250
Washington, DC 20001
Internet: www.newsguild.org

87. *Literary Agent*

DEFINITION

Literary agents sell potential employers on the creative talents of their clients.

TRANSFERABLE TEACHING SKILLS

- Strong written and oral communication skills
- Creative thinking
- Reasoning abilities

NECESSARY SKILLS

- Ability to recognize and cultivate marketable talent
- Experience in liberal arts, performing arts, and business administration
- Familiarity with the needs of publishers and potential employers

SUCCESS TIPS

- Be a problem solver
- Be a good negotiator
- Have a commanding vocabulary, to be persuasive

9 TO 5: HOW YOU WILL SPEND YOUR DAY

Literary agents have several responsibilities. Relationships with their clients generally fall into one of two categories: (1) ongoing and (2) case by case. Most literary agents have short-term relationships with clients, unless the client is a well-known, established author.

Because most prestigious newspapers and magazines won't consider any material unless an agent submits it, agents must be persistent in their search for literary talent. Editors rely on literary agents to thoroughly screen submissions in hopes that only the best available submissions reach their desks.

Literary agents also advise clients on negotiating contracts and are responsible for ensuring that clients receive compensation. Agents, in an effort to make sure writers stay on task, may also assist writers with such personal situations as preparing tax forms, bookkeeping, and processing income checks.

WHERE YOU WILL SPEND YOUR DAY

Most literary agents maintain regular office hours, but are often on call for meetings during evenings and on weekends with editors and potential clients. Beginning agents should expect modest office space, whereas more successful agents often enjoy spacious, elegant offices. Experienced, established agents might be required to travel across the globe in pursuit of their duties.

CAREER FORECAST

Work as a literary agent is extremely competitive and can result in high agent turnover with agencies within the field. Many agents are vying for very few jobs.

MONETARY REWARDS

Independent agents take a percentage of their clients' earnings (four to twenty percent), which affects their earnings. Agents who work out of agencies can earn between $20,000 and $60,000 per year.

Up the Ladder

Advancement comes from the agent's ability to be persistent, persuasive, and ambitious. Success depends greatly upon the agent gaining the trust of successful clients as key decision makers in the marketplace.

Related Jobs

- Property manager
- Food service manager
- Wholesale and retail buyer

Gathering More Facts

Association of Authors' Representatives, Inc
P.O. Box 237201
Ansonia Station
New York, NY 10003
Internet: www.publishersweekly.com/aar/

Independent Literary Agents Association (ILAA)
55 Fifth Avenue
New York, NY 10003

WritersNet
Internet: www.writers.net

88. *Proofreader*

Definition

A person who reads and checks submissions for errors.

Transferable Teaching Skills

- Meeting deadlines
- Enjoyment of reading
- Being detail-oriented

Necessary Skills

- Master's grasp of the English language
- Ability to communicate clearly
- Critical eye for organization and detail

Success Tips

- Organize ideas quickly
- Have computer applications knowledge, especially of word processors
- Make quick decisions

9 to 5: How You Will Spend Your Day

Proofreaders are responsible for reading and evaluating transcripts and manuscripts in search of any typographical, grammatical, or compositional mistakes. Some examples of what proofreaders search for are subject-verb disagreements, run-on sentences, and misspelled words. Some physical defects in a document may be alignment, indentation, or incorrect spacing.

Proofreaders may be required to work directly with editors, writers, or both, in an effort to assist in meeting the end the writer intended with the submission. Proofreaders may have to work within a deadline as well. Being able to do so quickly and efficiently will go a long way toward ensuring job security.

Where You Will Spend Your Day

Proofreaders, like most people in publishing, may have an office but are not restricted to work in it. Independent proofreaders and those with smaller businesses may have modest office space. More experienced proofreaders with larger businesses may have more spacious accommodations. Ultimately, proofreaders can accomplish as much work at home as they can in an office.

Career Forecast

Openings in this field are expected to decline through the year 2006. This is due in part to so much editing software being developed for word processing programs. However, computer software can't account for the human element that only trained proofreaders can provide.

Monetary Rewards

Proofreaders make from $10 to $25 an hour. With a consistent supply of work, proofreaders can expect to earn between $22,500 and $40,000 a year.

Up the Ladder

Advancement generally depends on the proofreader's reputation with employers and the ability to effectively handle publishing deadlines.

Related Jobs

- Editor
- Executive assistant
- Research assistant

From Classroom to . . .

As a junior high school English teacher, Maggie Henry spent her days teaching students how to proofread their work. She was very good at her job but loved the opportunity to work out of her home as a *freelance proofreader*. "You need the eyes of an eagle for this job. I spend my days in my home office, scrutinizing manuscripts and looking for typographical errors or any other inconsistencies on the printed page. I also check to see that copy from the printer exactly matches the manuscript. The additional training that I received by attending school has made my job easier."

GATHERING MORE FACTS

Editorial Freelance Association
72 West 23rd Street, Suite 154
New York, NY 10010
Phone (212) 929-5400

Freelance Editorial Association
P.O. Box 380835
Cambridge, MA 02238
Phone: (617) 729-8164

The Slot
Internet: www.theslot.com

89. *Resume Writer*

DEFINITION

Someone who writes resumes for individuals searching for jobs.

TRANSFERABLE TEACHING SKILLS

- Information gathering
- Writing
- Organizing information

NECESSARY SKILLS

- Keyboarding
- Listening
- Proofreading

SUCCESS TIPS

- Organize client information effectively
- Have a good eye for balance in the layout of the resume
- Have a strong grasp of word usage and vocabulary

9 TO 5: HOW YOU WILL SPEND YOUR DAY

Resume writers prepare resumes, which are summaries of the qualifications of someone looking for work. They must research the design most likely to attract potential employers' attention and then create resumes that make a quick, favorable impression through attractive packaging and key word usage. Some resume writers specialize in certain types of applications, such as executive resumes. These writers focus on using words and designs that exhibit traits desirable in these types of resumes.

WHERE YOU WILL SPEND YOUR DAY

Much as in other fields of writing, resume writers work where and when they want to work, whether they are at home or at a resume writing service. Hours can be part time or full time, depending upon the amount of work available.

CAREER FORECAST

This field is dwindling because of the number of resume books and computer programs available. However, specialization in resumes for highly competitive fields may prove lucrative.

MONETARY REWARDS

Resume writers usually charge $60 to $125 per resume. Those writers employed by resume services may earn commissions. Benefits are rarely provided.

UP THE LADDER

Advancement is in one of two forms, either more clients or an executive position in a service. Either form promises greater earnings.

Related Jobs

- Designer
- Proofreader
- Public relations specialist

Gathering More Facts

American Association for Career Education
2900 Amby Place
Hermosa Beach, CA 90254-2216
Phone: (310) 376-7378

International Association of Career Management
    Professionals
2400 East Arizona Biltmore Circle, Suite 2250
Phoenix, AZ 85016
Phone: (602) 381-0011

National Resume Writers Association
Phone: (888) 679-2444
Internet: www.nrwa.com

Professional Association of Resume Writers
1388 Brightwaters Boulevard, NE
St. Petersburg, FL 33704
Phone: (800) 822-7279
Internet: www.parw.com

90. *Scriptwriter*

Definition

Someone who writes scripts for television or films.

Transferable Teaching Skills

- Listening skills
- Writing ability
- Evaluation skills

Necessary Skills

- Ability to express ideas clearly
- Ability to develop original ideas
- Ability to develop a well-organized storyline

Success Tips

- Create characters who come to life
- Generate many ideas
- Be self-critical

9 to 5: How You Will Spend Your Day

Scriptwriters create scripts for dramas, comedies, soap operas, films, and advertisements. Content writers prepare station announcements, local shows, and local advertisements according to tight deadlines. Broadcasting scriptwriters write a specified amount daily for a particular audience at a designated time slot on the television, such as in a soap opera or drama series. Film scriptwriters and playwrights produce much larger, single works.

All scriptwriters must include stage directions and must be prepared to rewrite lines that actors find difficult. Scriptwriters are often part of large production teams, which rely upon them for success.

Where You Will Spend Your Day

Scriptwriters are free to write when and where they choose, as long as they meet deadlines. Travel to various sets may be necessary, or all writing could be done in the author's home. Hours of work depend upon deadlines.

Career Forecast

Competition is intense in this field, but novelty and creativity are always welcome in the entertainment industry.

MONETARY REWARDS

Television networks pay $2,000 to $5,000 a week to continuity writers; $5,000 to $20,000 for a thirty-minute script; and about $46,000 for a two-hour program. Film writers earn from $55,000 to $600,000 per successful script. Benefits are never included.

UP THE LADDER

Advancement depends upon the believable originality of the scriptwriter, and this results in higher pay.

RELATED JOBS

- Radio and television announcer
- Editor
- Technical writer

GATHERING MORE FACTS

Association of Authors' Representatives
10 Astor Place, Third Floor
New York, NY 10003
Phone: (212) 353-3709

American Screenwriters Association
269 S. Beverly Drive, Suite 2600
Beverly Hills, CA 90212-3807
Fax: (866) 265-9091
Internet: www.asascreenwriters.com

Writers Guild of America, West
7000 West Third Street
Los Angeles, CA 90048
Phone: (213) 951-4000

91. *Copywriter*

DEFINITION

A copywriter is the author of copy for production material and advertisements.

TRANSFERABLE TEACHING SKILLS

- Identifying errors
- Working quickly
- Following rules

NECESSARY SKILLS

- Handling pressure
- Technical know-how
- Flexibility

SUCCESS TIPS

- Enjoy reading
- Be able to spot errors
- Be able to make decisions

9 TO 5: HOW YOU WILL SPEND YOUR DAY

Copywriters create the mundane works many of us see in advertising, software, and other media. Copywriters are flexible in what they write; they're able to write technical software manuals immediately after creating advertisements. They begin by obtaining all necessary information and then consolidating this information into the desired format. They must work quickly to meet deadlines set by clients. Most copywriters are freelance writers.

WHERE YOU WILL SPEND YOUR DAY

Like most writers, copywriters work wherever and whenever they want, as long as they meet deadlines. Many operate their businesses from home, using computers, either as part-time or full-time work.

CAREER FORECAST

Aggressive marketing allows a copywriter much opportunity for employment. But salaried scriptwriters and technical writers are often preferred over copywriters.

MONETARY REWARDS

Earnings depend upon the amount of work. Yearly earnings for successful, full-time copywriters average from $50,000 to as much as $100,000.

UP THE LADDER

Advancement as a copywriter is only through the growth of a steady clientele, thus providing a greater income and job security.

RELATED JOBS

- Advertising
- Public relations specialist
- Proofreader

GATHERING MORE FACTS

Independent Writers of Southern California
P.O. Box 34279
Los Angeles, CA 90034
Phone: (877) 799-7483
Internet: www.iwosc.org

Society for Technical Communication
901 North Stuart Street, Suite 904
Arlington, VA 22203
Phone: (703) 522-4114
Internet: www.stc.org

The National Writers Union
113 University Place, 6th Floor
New York, NY 10003
Phone: (212) 254-0279
Internet: www.nwu.org

92. *Writer*

DEFINITION

Someone whose occupation is to write, either fiction or non-fiction.

TRANSFERABLE TEACHING SKILLS

- Creativity
- Organizing skills
- Ability to envision

NECESSARY SKILLS

- Ability to express ideas clearly
- Good general knowledge and research skills
- Initiative and good writing skills

SUCCESS TIPS

- Be self-disciplined
- Be articulate
- Generate many ideas

9 TO 5: HOW YOU WILL SPEND YOUR DAY

Every professional writer has essentially the same duties, regardless of what is being written. The first step in writing is the creation of an idea, either from personal creativity and interests or from assignments given by an editor. Once an idea is firmly grasped, it must be developed, either through research, analysis, or plot development, and it must then be placed in an outline form. Once an outline meets approval, the writer then proceeds to refine a number of drafts of the work until a final draft is acceptable to all.

WHERE YOU WILL SPEND YOUR DAY

Writers have perhaps the greatest flexibility in work hours and environment of all careers, provided deadlines are met. Work hours are usually 35 to 40 in number, but overtime is not uncommon. Writers work in whichever environment they write best, whether at home, in an office, or abroad at a foreign resort.

CAREER FORECAST

Although the demand for writers, particularly technical writers, is growing quickly, applicants far outnumber the available job openings.

MONETARY REWARDS

Earnings vary tremendously, depending upon the type of writing, the experience of the writer, and the amount of work undertaken. Benefits vary as much as earnings do.

UP THE LADDER

Advancement comes from successful writing in the form of more accepted works, more important assignments, or both. Earnings and benefits increase with advancement.

RELATED JOBS

- Editor
- Technical writer
- Reporter

GATHERING MORE FACTS

National Association of Science Writers
P.O. Box 294
Greenlawn, NY 11740
Phone: (516) 757-5664

National Conference of Editorial Writers
6223 Executive Boulevard
Rockville, MD 20852
Phone: (301) 984-3015
Internet: www.ncew.org

Poets and Writers
72 Spring Street
New York, NY 10012
Phone: (212) 226-3586
Internet: www.pw.org

Let the Games Begin!

I f you've always enjoyed sports and recreation, but you didn't become a physical education teacher or a coach, you're probably getting restless being confined to a classroom on a daily basis.

The careers in this chapter offer an opportunity to work in a gym or a park. Recreation is necessary for everyone who wants to lead a healthy life. Being a travel agent is a career option if you like to travel or plan vacations and getaways.

93. *Adventure Travel Specialist*

DEFINITION

Adventure travel specialists plan vacations for people who want to challenge their physical endurance.

TRANSFERABLE TEACHING SKILLS

- Critical thinking
- Listening skills
- Idea generation

Necessary Skills

- Knowledge of business, ecology, and social history
- Confidence in dealing with people and a passion for sharing a love of nature with others
- Good physical shape and a mature common sense
- Knowledge of emergency first aid

Success Tips

- Be physically fit
- Have strong leadership skills
- Exercise excellent problem-solving skills

9 to 5: How You Will Spend Your Day

Adventure travel specialists fulfill one or both of two aspects of adventure travel. Some specialists work only in an office environment, where they plan trip itineraries; arrange transportation, activity, and lodging reservations; and sell tour packages. Every aspect of the adventure travel tour must be planned in advance, including the supply of equipment and guides. Some specialists are essentially field-workers, usually called outfitters. They oversee and guide the travelers on their tour. The outfitters are directly responsible for the safety of the clients when touring. They may have to demonstrate or assist in clients' activities. Outfitters may also act as ecological or historical commentators. Adventure travel specialists may serve as both planners and outfitters, particularly in smaller tour operations.

Where You Will Spend Your Day

Adventure travel specialists do most of their work in comfortable, air-conditioned offices. Most of these specialists still have to spend some time in the field to gain an understanding of how to plan tours.

Career Forecast

Although the adventure segment of the travel industry is small, it is growing, as more people take activity-oriented vacations to explore the environment and test their physical endurance.

Monetary Rewards

Earnings depend upon weather conditions and vacation seasons, as well as on the overall condition of the economy. An outfitter can make about $17,000 for a three- to four-month period. Managers may make as much as $65,000 per year.

Up the Ladder

For office-bound planners, advancement is in the form of increased responsibilities and higher pay. Outfitters usually find advancement in guiding more tours.

Related Jobs

- Flight attendant
- Travel agent
- Park ranger

Gathering More Facts

Professional Guides Association of America
2416 South Eads Street
Arlington, VA 22202

The Adventure Travel Society
6551 South Revere Parkway, Suite 160
Englewood, CO 80111
Phone: (303) 649-9016

The Outdoor Recreation Coalition of America
P.O. Box 1319
Boulder, CO 80306

Phone: (303) 444-3353
E-mail: info@orca.org
Internet: www.orca.org

94. *Athletic Coach*

DEFINITION

An athletic coach is responsible for the preparation and performance of an athletic team.

TRANSFERABLE TEACHING SKILLS

- Developing
- Motivating
- Preparing

NECESSARY SKILLS

- People skills
- Supervisory talents
- Good communication

SUCCESS TIPS

- Be able to work with a group
- Know the rules
- Have a love of the sport

9 TO 5: HOW YOU WILL SPEND YOUR DAY

The first part of the athletic coach's job is to choose the players for the team, unless the coach works with athletes who
compete individually, as in golf and tennis. In this case, the
athletes come to the coach. Typically, though, the athletic
coach for a team must be able to either scout talented athletes

or sort out scouting reports on athletes, in order to build a competitive team.

Once the team is constructed, the coach must help the players work together to understand and operate the plays and strategies that the coach deems necessary to be competitive. This aspect of coaching involves more than physical preparation of the athletes; it also involves mental preparation to ensure that they do not defeat their abilities with negativity.

Smaller teams may require their coaches to perform administrative tasks, such as equipment maintenance, facility reservation, and practice scheduling. A coach's primary responsibility is to the players, however, as their caretakers and their teachers.

Where You Will Spend Your Day

Coaches who work with individually competitive athletes typically do so in a camp, club, or clinic designed for that purpose. Team coaches work long hours in the institution sponsoring their teams, whether colleges, high schools, or some other sponsor. Team coaches often must travel far to accompany their teams on away games.

Career Forecast

Many new sports teams are forming, but competition is fierce for the limited number of coaching positions.

Monetary Rewards

Earnings vary so widely that no estimate can be given. Earnings are dependent upon location and coaching success.

Up the Ladder

Advancement, in the form of coaching larger teams or better-known athletes, depends almost entirely upon the success of the athletes you have previously coached.

Related Jobs

- Athletic director
- Athletic trainer
- Recreational therapist

Gathering More Facts

American Coaching Association
P.O. Box 353
Lafayette Hill, PA 19444
Phone: (610) 825-4505
Internet: www.americoach.com

American Council on Exercise
4851 Paramount Drive
San Diego, CA 92123

From Classroom to . . .

Lane Wimer has been coaching for twenty-three years. He started out coaching an eighth-grade boys' basketball team when he taught middle school and later coached boys' high school basketball. "I heard about a college looking for an assistant *coach* and decided to apply for that position. I gained a lot of experience from it and was offered the head coach's position several years later.

"While the job can be time-consuming, it's quite rewarding to know that I am a positive influence on these young men. I think you have to be a good communicator to be able to motivate and teach players the technical and tactical side of the game. The best coaches have superior leadership and organizational skills, as well as patience. Coaching is a lot like teaching, because a coach is always teaching new things like plays or strategies and helping the player discover and use his true potential."

Phone: (800) 825-3636
Internet: www.acefitness.org

National High School Athletic Coaches Association
P.O. Box 4342
Hamden, CT 06514
Internet: www.hscoaches.org

95. *Recreation Worker*

DEFINITION

Recreation workers help people enjoy recreational activities.

TRANSFERABLE TEACHING SKILLS

- Overseeing
- Coaching
- Scheduling

NECESSARY SKILLS

- Creativity
- Management ability
- Good communication

SUCCESS TIPS

- Be in good physical shape
- Enjoy getting people involved
- Be organized

9 TO 5: HOW YOU WILL SPEND YOUR DAY

Companies employ recreation workers for various reasons. Hospitals use recreation workers to assist physicians in planning patients' activities. Industry employs recreational workers to coordinate recreational events and social gatherings. Other places, such as correctional facilities, nonprofit youth organizations, schools, and day-care centers, also employ recreation workers.

There are basically four types of recreation workers. Recreation leaders instruct groups of people in recreational activities such as sports and dancing. Recreation directors monitor recreation leaders. They also are responsible for getting new equipment and securing funds from government sources. Camp counselors instruct and supervise campers in skills such as canoeing and water skiing. Activity specialists are responsible for teaching one specific skill. An activity specialist may teach swimming or coach basketball.

WHERE YOU WILL SPEND YOUR DAY

Most recreation workers work 40-hour weeks, but can expect to work nights, weekends, and irregular hours. The locale for a recreation worker could be a playground, a hospital, or a cruise ship. Recreation workers spend most of their time outdoors and may be required to work in unfavorable weather conditions. Recreation directors spend most of their time planning events.

CAREER FORECAST

The employment outlook is promising through the year 2006. Increased earnings, more leisure time, and improved recreation facilities have all created an increased demand for adequate leisure facilities. Because much of the recreational work is seasonal, many recreation workers are employed part time. Competition for full-time positions will be fierce. Workers with more experience and training will have the best chance for employment in this field.

MONETARY REWARDS

Full-time recreation workers earn an average salary of $13,000 to $29,000 a year. Directors and supervisors earn considerably more. Benefits vary, depending on the employer, location, and experience of the worker.

Up the Ladder

Mainly, advancement for recreation workers involves moving from the position of recreation worker to that of recreation director. With experience and further education, recreation leaders can make themselves available for prestigious, better-paying administrative positions.

Related Jobs

- Counseling psychologist
- School counselor
- Social worker

Gathering More Facts

American Council on Exercise
4851 Paramount Drive
San Diego, CA 92123
Phone: (800) 825-3636
Internet: www.acefitness.org

Employee Services Management Association
2211 York Road, Suite 207
Oak Park, IL 60523-2371
Phone: (630) 368-1280
Internet: www.esmassn.org

National Recreation and Park Association
22377 Belmont Ridge Road
Ashburn, VA 20148-4501
Phone: (703) 858-0784
Internet: www.nrpa.org/nrpa

96. *Naturalist*

DEFINITION

Naturalists study nature by observing the environment.

TRANSFERABLE TEACHING SKILLS

- Love of science
- Love of the outdoors
- Verbalization skills

NECESSARY SKILLS

- Scientific background
- Technical knowledge
- Good communication

SUCCESS TIPS

- Be an investigator
- Oversee all aspects of the environment
- Be able to inform

9 TO 5: HOW YOU WILL SPEND YOUR DAY

The global spread of humanity has made an indelible mark upon the environment in nearly every part of the world. Our nation's flora and fauna would be seriously harmed by this encroachment if it were not for the efforts of naturalists. They help wildlife improve its chances of survival in the midst of a world dominated by humanity. Several types of naturalists exist, such as fish and wildlife officers, wildlife managers, range managers, and conservationists.

Fish and wildlife officers study and regulate the populations of fish, hunted animals, and protected and endangered animals. They control hunting and fishing, and they target and arrest poachers. Wildlife managers, range managers, and conservationists maintain wildlife in particular areas. Wildlife managers work in local and national parks. Range managers work in areas that have livestock and wildlife living side by side. Conservationists are basically lobbyists concerned about nature.

Naturalists typically have administrative duties over staff, funds, and records, and they must maintain public relations through editorials, books, and interviews. Naturalists usually attempt to educate the public through nature walks, bird watching, demonstrations, park exhibits, and conservation classes.

WHERE YOU WILL SPEND YOUR DAY

Field naturalists typically spend most of their time outside in the natural environment. Those in supervisory positions may be too occupied with administrative duties to be found in the natural environment they oversee. Naturalists usually work 35 to 40 hours per week, although overtime may be necessary during camping seasons, storms, and burn seasons.

CAREER FORECAST

Although public concern about the environment is growing, government cutbacks and an increasing number of applicants make for heavy competition in this limited field.

MONETARY REWARDS

Salaries range from $15,000 to $70,000 per year, depending on the level of administrative responsibilities. Benefits include housing, vehicles, and health insurance.

UP THE LADDER

Advancement is only possible in large organizations, where naturalists with experience and at least a graduate degree can advance to administrative positions.

RELATED JOBS

- Ecologist
- Park ranger
- Zoologist

GATHERING MORE FACTS

Environmental Careers Organization
286 Congress Street, 3rd Floor
Boston, MA 02210-1-38
Phone: (617) 426-4375

Forest Service
U.S. Department of Agriculture
Sidney R. Yates Federal Building
201 14th Street, SW at Independence Avenue, SW
Washington, DC 20250
Phone: (202) 205-1680
Internet: www.fs.fed.us

From Classroom to . . .

Joanne Landin is an *interpreter* at a Department of Natural Resources reservoir park. "As a teenager, I worked part time at the reservoir helping to maintain the park. I returned to the park as an interpreter after earning my teacher's degree and teaching for seven years. Now I develop and lead programs for schools visiting the reservoir on field trips. I help the children identify plants and animals found at the reservoir and teach them the importance of preserving the environment for the well-being of our planet. I'm still very much a teacher, only I teach in an outdoor classroom."

Natural Wildlife Federation
8925 Leesburg Pike
Vienna, VA 22184
Phone: (718) 790-4000
Internet: www.nwf.org

97. *Park Ranger*

DEFINITION

Park rangers enforce laws and protect county, state, and national parks.

TRANSFERABLE TEACHING SKILLS

- Inspecting
- Discovering
- Analyzing

NECESSARY SKILLS

- Must have excellent leadership skills
- Must enjoy helping others
- Must be physically fit

SUCCESS TIPS

- Enjoy the outdoors
- Be able to know when something is wrong
- Have a knowledge of wildlife

9 TO 5: HOW YOU WILL SPEND YOUR DAY

Park rangers are responsible for various tasks in our nation's parks. Their number-one priority is the safety of the people who visit the parks, the wild and plant life within the park, and the park itself. They are responsible for collecting registration and park fees and registering vehicles visiting the park. They enforce laws and policies that govern our national parks. Park rangers also assist fire fighters and rescue workers in the event of forest fires.

Park rangers are responsible for the care and management of exotic and native animal species found in our national parks. Rangers may be called upon to research information relevant to the protection of the environment that offers crucial support to park wildlife.

One final responsibility of park rangers is to make visitors' trips to our national parks as enjoyable as possible. This is accomplished through guided tours, lectures, and personal attention.

WHERE YOU WILL SPEND YOUR DAY

Rangers work in parks all across the county, from Alaska to Colorado to Florida. They generally work 40-hour weeks, but there is a great deal of overtime. Because of park rangers' many responsibilities, they are on call twenty-four hours a day.

CAREER FORECAST

The job outlook for park rangers is not very promising. Competition for positions is fierce and expected to remain so indefinitely. The U.S. Park Service estimates that the number of applicants to available openings may be as high as 100 to 1.

MONETARY REWARDS

Salaries for park rangers vary, mainly due to experience. Annual salaries for rangers in national parks range from $18,000 to $28,000. Many parks provide housing for rangers who work in remote areas. They receive decent benefits, including health and life insurance, paid holidays and vacations, pension plans, and sick leave.

Up the Ladder

Most rangers start out in entry-level positions. This means that promotion is generally done within parks. Advancement for park rangers is promotion to park or district manager. They may also become experts in park planning and resource management.

Related Jobs

- Corrections officer
- Fire marshal
- Fish and game warden

Gathering More Facts

National Association of State Park Directors
9894 East Hidden Place
Tucson, AZ 85748
Phone: (520) 298-4924

National Parks and Conservation Association
1776 Massachusetts Avenue, NW
Washington, DC 20036
Phone: (202) 223-6722
Internet: www.npca.org/npca

National Recreation and Park Association
22377 Belmont Ridge Road
Ashburn, VA 20148-4510
Phone: (703) 858-0784
Internet: www.nrpa.org

98. *Activity Director*

Definition

An activity director provides activity programming for individuals or groups seeking to improve their quality of life or general recreation.

Transferable Teaching Skills

- Implementing new ideas
- Organizing
- Adapting ideas for a variety of individual needs

Necessary Skills

- Leadership
- High energy level
- Strong interpersonal skills

Success Tips

- Cultivate a charismatic personality
- Pursue additional education
- Maintain multiple activities at once

9 to 5: How You Will Spend Your Day

Activity directors are responsible for planning and implementing activity programming for the elderly or disabled in group homes, senior centers, nursing-care facilities, retirement homes/communities, or adult day-care facilities. They also plan activity programs for recreation centers, campgrounds, cruise ships, resorts, hotels, schools, and parks.

Activity directors who work with elderly clients plan, schedule, and supervise activities that support or enhance their well-being. These activities are not only recreational, but also therapeutic, and include fitness and exercise classes to help individuals keep physically fit. Activity directors may plan trips to a variety of destinations, such as shopping centers, museums, restaurants, sporting events, or other places of interest. Social events such as bridge clubs, speakers' or lecturers' series, and even dances contribute to the social enhancement of residents' lives. When planning these events, the activities director must take into consideration individuals' limitations by adapting plans to their capabilities.

Activity directors who work for campgrounds, cruise ships, hotels, resorts, and parks plan events that include swimming, team sports, picnics, bowling, skating, or sightseeing trips. The events include people of all ages—from the very young to retirees. Often, families want to take part in events in which they can participate as a family. Resort directors may include hunting or fishing expeditions for the sportsman. Being able to oversee and maintain several activities at once is an important asset for activity directors. Some directors may have a staff to lead the activities.

WHERE YOU WILL SPEND YOUR DAY

Many activity directors will work directly with the residents or guests. Therefore, they may be in a variety of settings throughout the day: a shopping center, a sports stadium, or in the woods, leading a hunting expedition. Activity directors usually have an office where they can complete paperwork or reports, plan activities, or perform other administrative duties.

CAREER FORECAST

Nursing-care facilities will need more activity directors as their populations increase because of the aging baby boomer generation. Opportunities for resort, cruise ship, and hotel activity directors are expected to grow slowly, but this is sensitive to changes in the economy.

MONETARY REWARDS

Earnings for activity directors vary, according to experience, location, and the employer. Average annual earnings for resort and hotel activity directors, as well as for a director for parks, is $21,500. Activity directors for nursing-care facilities and senior citizen communities earn on average between $25,200 and $31,600. These directors are often certified recreation professionals, which enables them to demand a higher wage.

UP THE LADDER

Advancement includes moving into supervisory or management positions. Some activity directors go into business for themselves and consult with businesses or facilities that want to create activity programs. Continuing education or additional certification can lead to advancement in pay or position.

RELATED JOBS

- Resort manager
- City recreation director
- Personal trainer

GATHERING MORE FACTS

American Alliance for Health, Physical Education,
    Recreation, and Dance
1900 Association Drive
Reston, VA 20191-1598
Phone: (800) 213-7193
Internet: www.aahperd.org

American Association for Leisure and
    Recreation (AALR)
1900 Association Drive
Reston, VA 20191
Phone: (703) 476-3472
Internet: www.aahperd.org/aalr

American Council on Exercise
4851 Paramount Drive
San Diego, CA 92123
Phone: (800) 825-3636
Internet: www.acefitness.org

99. *Sports Management Professional*

DEFINITION

Sports management professionals direct and oversee the management, marketing, and supervisory functions of sports-related organizations.

TRANSFERABLE TEACHING SKILLS

- Motivation
- Supervising skills
- Organizing

NECESSARY SKILLS

- Creativity
- Management skills
- Enthusiasm

SUCCESS TIPS

- Be able to work with people
- Be visionary—able to know what the team needs
- Maintain what you've accomplished and help your clients maintain their successful performance

9 TO 5: HOW YOU WILL SPEND YOUR DAY

Many opportunities exist for sports management professionals, in places ranging from professional sports franchises to schools and churches with athletic programs. Sports management professionals have various titles and responsibilities. Promotion and developmental directors are responsible for promotional campaigns designed to sell season ticket packages. Sports advertising managers work alongside promotion and development to supervise the promotion of individual sports figures, teams, or athletic programs. They are also responsible for securing deals from advertisers for sporting events.

Sports information directors are a go-between for sports figures or teams and the news media. They provide press guides and organize media access to the athletes. They also create team or athletic publications, which could be informational brochures or Web sites. Athletic directors and general managers are responsible for the daily activities of the team. They make decisions on personnel hiring and firing and oversee employees of sports facilities. Athletic directors report to university heads, and general managers report to team managers. They negotiate playing or coaching contracts, arrange product endorsement, and supply financial advice.

Where You Will Spend Your Day

State-of-the-art offices are usually where sports management professionals conduct their daily business. Regular 40-hour weeks are rare, due to the sports professional's constant need to travel with the team or sports figure. This, however, can be viewed as an excellent perk for sports fans.

Career Forecast

This is considered a glamorous profession, and competition is intense. Employment opportunities are expected to increase, as sports become a more dominant entertainment outlet in our society.

Monetary Rewards

Earnings vary widely, depending on the value of the team, the institution, or individual athletes. Sports administrators working for school districts earn starting salaries of about $19,000, but these increase to an average of $44,000 after ten years of service. The average salary for sports advertising managers is $78,300 annually. Athletic directors could earn more or less, depending on their institution of employment. Sports agents' earnings depend on their number of clients and their percentage (usually 3 to 4 percent) of their client's income.

Up the Ladder

Sports are a huge, booming business and the advancement possibilities are extensive. Advancement could mean moving to a small community college or to a prestigious NCAA university as an athletic director. You could represent a local minor league prospect or an all-star baseball player as a sports agent.

Related Jobs

- Health service administrator
- Museum director
- Recreation and park manager

Gathering More Facts

American Management Association
1601 Broadway
New York, NY 10019-7240
Internet: www.amamet.org

Association of Representatives of Professional Athletes
100000 Santa Monica Boulevard, Suite 312
Century City, CA 90067

National Association of Sports Officials
2017 Lathrop Avenue
Racine, WI 53405
Phone: (414) 632-5448

100. *Travel Agent*

Definition

Travel agents aid people or groups with travel plans or other related tasks.

TRANSFERABLE TEACHING SKILLS

- Organizational ability
- Good people skills
- Listening skills

NECESSARY SKILLS

- Good communication
- Efficiency
- Honesty

SUCCESS TIPS

- Be persistent
- Hunt out the best deals
- Manage your clients' time wisely

9 TO 5: HOW YOU WILL SPEND YOUR DAY

Travel agents are salespeople specializing in bookkeeping, organizing trips and tours, and traveling consultation. If they are self-employed, they are responsible for all of these duties. If they are part of an office setting, different agents may be responsible for specific areas, ranging from luxury trips to vacations in the Caribbean. Travel agents use various sources for information on hotel rates and accommodations, air rates, and plane arrival and departure times.

Travel agents often make suggestions to clients on hotel rates, alternative transportation plans, and itineraries. They provide information about foreign current exchange, customer regulations, visa and passport regulations, travelers' checks, and accident and baggage insurance.

Travel agents also work as bookkeepers, handling various details of the trip. In this capacity, travel agents work with organizations such as airlines and car rental companies. They work as tour guides, heading trips to exotic destinations around the world, for anywhere from one to six weeks.

WHERE YOU WILL SPEND YOUR DAY

Travel agents generally work in an office, where the atmosphere is extremely competitive for customers. Work is usually conducted in-office, but some travel agents are required to work in the field. Most agents work a 40-hour week, including half days on Saturdays. Overtime may be necessary between January and June, which is the busy season. Agents who work overtime receive salaries or compensated time off.

CAREER FORECAST

The outlook for this career depends greatly on the state of the economy. There is expected steady growth, as more Americans travel abroad for business and pleasure. One factor that may hinder growth is travelers making their own travel plans through Internet services. This would in effect decrease the need for travel agencies.

MONETARY REWARDS

Travel agents generally earn a straight salary, plus commission. Salaries range from $16,400 to $24,500 annually. Agents with five or ten years' experience earn $26,300 to $32,6000 annually.

UP THE LADDER

Advancement is limited. Successful experienced agents may eventually be able to hire employees or establish their own offices.

RELATED JOBS

- Insurance agent
- Meeting planner
- Traveler counselor

From Classroom to . . .

Tabitha Givens has been a *travel agent* for more than ten years. After graduating from college with a degree in English and teaching high school, she did quite a bit of traveling during her summer breaks. She became interested in a career as a travel agent. "I took some community college classes to help me prepare for being a travel agent. My client base is mostly corporate accounts, but I also help individuals with travel packages. I really enjoy being a travel agent because I can help people make their trips and vacations more manageable by taking care of the details for them. I also enjoy the many opportunities I have to travel and learn more about the places my clients may want to travel to."

GATHERING MORE FACTS

American Society of Travel Agents
1101 King Street, Suite 200
Alexandria, VA 22314
Phone: (703) 739-2782
Internet: www.astanet.com

Association of Retail Travel Agents
1745 Jefferson Davis Highway, Suite 300
Arlington, VA 22202

Institute of Certified Travel Agents
P.O. Box 812059
148 Linden Street
Wellesley, MA 02482-0012
Phone: (800) 542-4282
Internet: www.iccta.com

101. *Personal Trainer*

DEFINITION

A personal trainer provides assistance with exercise, weight training, diet and nutrition, and weight loss for people who are health-conscious.

TRANSFERABLE TEACHING SKILLS

- Active listening
- Problem identification
- Speaking

NECESSARY SKILLS

- Physical fitness
- Adaptability
- Ability to work one-on-one with clients

SUCCESS TIPS

- Identify the nature of the problem
- Identify essential information
- Talk to others to effectively convey information

9 TO 5: HOW YOU WILL SPEND YOUR DAY

Personal trainers may have several different types of clients. They may be business executives or celebrities whose schedules are so busy, they only have time to work with a personal trainer. A client may be an aspiring or ex-athlete seeking specific sports-related training. The client may be an expectant mother trying to stay healthy during her pregnancy. In any case, personal trainers are entrusted with the physical, and in some cases mental, conditioning of their clients.

Some trainers choose to specialize in certain areas of physical training. Athletic trainers, for example, assist athletes in preparing for sports activities and help with the treatment of sports injuries.

No matter what area or type of physical training you focus on, you must be well informed in your craft. Trainers are called upon to help clients develop fitness goals and to design an exercise program to create those results. Trainers must be able to demonstrate the recommended exercises and offer support and encouragement for their clients' efforts and progress. Trainers also need to have a critical eye to recognize clients' strengths and weaknesses.

WHERE YOU WILL SPEND YOUR DAY

Personal trainers conduct their business mainly in exercise rooms or gyms. However, because of various client situations, workout sessions could take place in homes, offices, and even hotels. Generally, where the workout is done tends to be very flexible. Because most of the work is one-on-one, work hours are also more flexible than traditional workouts.

CAREER FORECAST

The career outlook for personal trainers is excellent. There will always be people who are concerned with getting healthier. For many, the issue of health is personal, and they require an individual approach to their situation. Personal trainers with excellent communication skills fit the bill.

MONETARY REWARDS

Personal trainers are usually paid by the hour, based on their experience and reputation. Most trainers receive hourly wages of between $20 and $30. More experienced, successful trainers can make up to $200 an hour. A trainer's yearly salary depends on the number of clients and hourly rates, minus the cost to advertise—if that is necessary. Because most trainers work for themselves, they are responsible for their own benefits.

Up the Ladder

Personal trainers may start with a modest clientele. Through hard work and success, that clientele may grow. Some trainers expand their services by becoming consultants, starting fitness centers, supervising other trainers, or creating audiotapes and writing books about fitness.

Related Jobs

- Athletic coach
- Franchise owner
- Physical therapist

Gathering More Facts

American Alliance for Health, Physical Education,
    Recreation, and Dance
1900 Association Drive
Reston, VA 20191-1598

From Classroom to . . .

"I love putting on my workout clothes and going to my job!" says Kathy Eberts, a *personal trainer*. Kathy no longer teaches kids to add and subtract, but she does teach people how to take care of their bodies. She hasn't always been a fitness fanatic, though. "After I lost seventy-five pounds, I wanted to help others feel good about themselves by improving their bodies in the correct way. I get the opportunity to instruct fitness groups, as well as individuals. It's very rewarding to see people excited about the transformation of their bodies because of their fitness program."

Phone: (800) 213-7193
Internet: www.aahperd.org

National Athletic Trainers Association
2952 Stemmons Freeway, Suite 200
Dallas, TX 75247-6103
Phone: (214) 637-6282

National Strength and Condition Association
P.O. Box 38909
Colorado Springs, CO 80937
Phone: (719) 632-6722
Internet: www.nsca-lift.org

CHAPTER TWELVE

Developing the Plan

Updating Your Resume

Okay: So you have read chapters 1 through 11 and have identified careers that match your skills. Keep in mind that you must take more steps to fully implement your plan. Just having confidence in your qualifications will not be enough. Your resume is the key to obtaining an interview for the job you desire.

Have you taken a close look at your resume? Remember that you no longer want a teaching career and that your old resume was probably written to help you land the fabulous teaching job that you now want to leave. A good resume should be written for each particular job that you apply for. Don't panic if you're planning to apply for different types of jobs or careers. Only minor adaptations may be necessary to custom-fit your resume to each particular job.

The real purpose of the resume is to "whet the employer's appetite." The key is presenting your information concisely and effectively enough to "market" yourself in an appealing manner. Don't tell your life story, and don't volunteer too much information. Your goal is for the prospective employer to like your credentials well enough to call and set up a face-to-face interview. If, however, a phone-screening interview is required, always be cooperative, listen attentively, be prepared to "sell" yourself, and remember not to volunteer information that wasn't requested. If the job sounds appealing, remember that it's often advisable for you, the candidate, to request a face-to-face interview before the call ends. If this approach sounds too aggressive, keep in mind that you can always say no at any time or withdraw from considering any particular position. As long as you wish to pursue a particular job, though, the employer needs to know that you are interested.

Your resume must be neatly arranged and your information in logical order on one page. If you feel you have enough applicable information for two pages, fine, but two pages is the maximum. Look closely at the resume on the following pages and see if you can determine which corrections are necessary before this resume is ready for submission. You will see a list of do's and don'ts following the resume.

1234 Main Street
Indianapolis, IN 40001 212-555-9631
mmg123@aol.com

Megan Gilman

PERSONAL INFORMATION
Married and mother of four children. Age 47, Height 5'6', weight 145 lbs., blond hair and green eyes.

OBJECTIVE
To obtain a management position earning over $50,000.00 per year. Long term objective is to own and manage my own business.

EXPERIENCE
More than 25 years of classroom teaching experience from kindergarten through college including adult basic education. Leadership roles as Literacy Coordinator at a local prison facility. Assistant Director of the Butler University Reading Center, Title One Reading Consultant, and national education speaker.

PRESENTATIONS
KAACE Fall 200 Literacy Conference, October 4, 5 & 6
   "Do You Know How Well You Read?"
Laubach International Conference in Orlando, Florida, June 8, 9,
   10, & 11   "Literacy a Pathway to Freedom"
Kentucky Association for Adult and Continuing Education, October
   1999

EDUCATION
Special Education degree completed in July of 2000
Administration—1997
Ed.S, Reading—Butler University 1977
M.S., Elementary Education and Reading—Butler University, 1971
Bachelors of Science in Elementary Education—Ball State
   University, 1969

LICENCES

License Reading Specialist, 1993 #123456-1999 #987651
Serious Emotionally Handicapped, added to life license,
    October 2000 Life #160271
Elementary Administration and Supervision Issued, 1999 #001100
General Elementary—Life #112233

AWARDS

Children's Reading Roundtable Award for Midwest Authors, 1986
Region III Correctional Educator of the Year May 2000 (Indiana,
    Michigan, Kentucky, Illinois, Ohio, and Wisconsin)
EDUCATOR'S Award, Indiana Department of Corrections, 1998
Great Efforts in Education/Hoosier Hero, Channel 6 News ABC,
    1999
Indiana Correctional Educator of the Year April, 2000

SPECIAL SKILLS

Good Computer Skills—can use Micro Soft Word, Excel, and
    Power Point
Certified Laubach Tutor-Trainer
Certified Red Cross Water Safety Instructor
Certified Red Cross First Aid Trainer
Knitting
Swimming
Tennis
Just learning golf
Good moral religious woman
SKY DIVING

REFERENCES

Mark Miller personal family friend and owner of his own business.
    555-348-1225
Charles Stiles colleague and Laubach Literacy national trainer.
    555-354-9876
Edda Fisher current boss
    555-789-5555

* * *

What errors were you able to find in the previous resume? (See pages 325–26 and also refer to Do's and Don'ts sections.)

Do

- Keep resume to one or two full pages.
- Never include a picture.
- Make sure the size of type is legible.
- Proof, spell check, and reread for errors.
- Make sure margins are equal.
- Make sure your name appears on each page.
- Stay consistent with:
  - Size of type
  - Style of type or font
  - Use of bold, underlining, and capitalization
  - Spacing
  - Using tabs and indentations
- Don't volunteer unnecessary personal information: age, marital status, number of children, height, weight, religious affiliation, and so forth.
- Stating an objective is fine, especially because you're seeking to change careers. However, don't assume you will obtain a management position; don't specify a salary desired; and don't offer a long-term objective if it indicates that you're planning yet another career move.
- Summarizing your experience in paragraph form is acceptable. However, a chronological listing of employment that identifies responsibilities for each particular position you have held is preferred. This format is easier to read and quicker to interpret.
- Don't volunteer your years' experience beyond the number ten. Seldom will an employer seek more than ten years of experience in any area.
- When listing items in a certain category, arrange them in chronological order, with the most recent item first.
- Don't volunteer activities that may be viewed as too risky.

- Listing references is acceptable, so long as you have prepared those people for receiving a call regarding your search.
- Only list your current employer as a reference if you are 100 percent certain that this won't jeopardize your current employment.

Don't

- Include your picture or a photo of any kind.
- Use too many different styles or sizes of type.
- Offer personal information such as height, weight, hair or eye color, race, marital status, number of children, religion, date of birth, financial status, limiting disabilities, or spouse's occupation.
- Use a career objective that is too narrow in its focus. Keep in mind that you should change the objective when you apply to each particular job.
- List references, even though you feel they may be very impressive.
- Include salary information or salary history.
- Volunteer dates of your degrees if you are self-conscious about your age.
- Include a GPA under 3.0, unless you can justify that extracurricular activities, employment, or both of these affected your academic performance.
- Specify that you are seeking part-time or full-time employment, if you are truly open to either.
- Overuse different colors of type.

The following Do's and Don'ts will help ensure that you create a professional resume.

Do

- Space the information neatly on the page.
- Spell check and have a friend or colleague proofread the resume for grammar and punctuation.
- Include a home mailing address, a phone number, and e-mail addresses. Include cellular phone, work phones, work

e-mail addresses *only* if you're confident that receiving calls at work will not jeopardize your current employment.
- Include work history in reverse chronological order, listing most recent or current employment first. Remember to include dates, and if presently employed, indicate so.
- List your educational experiences in reverse chronological order and include GPA if 3.0 or better. Specify that you have received a particular degree and state the college or university.
- Include training, seminars, workshops, conferences, and certifications and list in reverse chronological order, including dates.
- Include at least your name, if not other contact information, on the top of the second page of a two-page resume. This is to avoid any confusion if the pages get separated.
- Make use of bold type, underlining, or italics to highlight things such as your name, headings, or position titles. Be careful not to overuse these.
- Bring attention to awards, certificates of achievements, and other honors that will help distinguish you from other candidates.
- Include activities and leadership positions, such as president of your class, lead teacher, department chair, committee chair, and so forth.
- Include community involvement, such as chairing the United Way Funding Committee, vice-president of the Chamber of Commerce, chairperson of United Way, school board member.
- Include a summary of skills section below your objective, identifying transferable skills, talents, and experiences that indicate your suitability for a new career.
- Include an objective that is specific for the job applied for.
- Use white or light-colored paper, as opposed to dark or bold color.

The following resume incorporates many of the elements listed in the "Do" list. You can use this example as a guide when you update your resume.

Stephen K. Whiting
3702 Stonehedge Place, Apt. 1E
Indianapolis, IN 46240
(317) 555-9124
skw01@aol.com

OBJECTIVE

My objective is to secure an executive sales position with a firm committed to success, with the opportunity for advancement.

EMPLOYMENT

Director of Sales   March 1999–present

Sales Engineer   (March 1999–December 1999)

ABC Company; Indianapolis, IN

ABC represents a number of industrial weighing and force measurement equipment manufacturers. Responsibilities include sales, system design, project management, and customer relations for the State of Indiana. Extremely successful at increasing sales, developing customer rapport, expanding customer base, and overall territory management.

- Increased sales 140% in first year
- Consistently exceeded monthly sales quota
- Acquired more than 40 new customers through aggressive sales tactics
- Achieved largest month in company for 1999 and 2000
- Established most extensive customer database in company history (more than 1,400 customers/contacts)
- Achieved 120% of 1998 sales quota
- Performed all Chatillon software demonstrations and installations throughout Indiana
- Developed key accounts such as Depuy, Firestone, Delco, Remy, Meijer, and Conseco

Annuity Analyst   July 1997–March 1999

Conseco, Inc.; Carmel, IN

- Traveled with a team of acquisition experts to learn about each acquired company's product portfolio

- Responsible for maintaining more than 150,000 annuity accounts over four different companies
- Handled all new business transactions
- Trained new employees and implemented "quality committees" to improve departmental performance

EDUCATION

Bachelor of Science Degree in Public Management;
Indiana University, Bloomington, IN; 1996

INTERESTS / ACTIVITIES

- Member of Lambda Chi Alpha Fraternity
- Received outstanding rush performance award
- Internal Social Chairman
- Volunteered for Meals on Wheels Program

* * *

Tips for a Successful Interview

Your cover letter and resume will help you get an interview. An interview helps you get the job, and good interview skills help you beat out the competition. Here are some Do's and Don'ts to ensure that you perform well in an interview.

Do

- Be prompt. In fact, be 15 minutes early.
- Approach the interview in a positive manner, keeping a good attitude, enthusiasm, and interest level throughout the entire process.
- Offer a firm handshake.
- Take extra resumes and any other appropriate documents, including examples of your work, a list of references with contact information, letters of recommendation, certificates of achievement, copies of diplomas, transcripts, and so forth.
- Dress appropriately from head to toe for each interview. You are usually wise to dress conservatively, as opposed to

casually. Also, follow the rule of thumb to be at least as well dressed as the interviewer, if not better.

- Cover all visible tattoos and remove all visible piercing.
- Be well groomed. You are safest to remove all facial hair. However, if you must keep your mustache, beard, or goatee, make sure that it is neatly trimmed.
- Make sure that your hair is neat, clean, and styled appropriately.
- Be cooperative and patient throughout the whole interviewing process. Remember that hiring employees may be only a small part of that particular day's duties for the interviewer.
- Treat each follow-up interview with an employer as "a whole new ball game." Don't assume that because you are invited for a second or third interview, you "have the job." Be prepared to answer the same questions and have your interest level tested by different interviewers from the same organization.
- Listen attentively throughout the interviewing process.
- Keep good eye contact with whomever you are speaking.
- Interrupt yourself if you feel that you are rambling and have lost the interviewer's attention. Stop and ask the interviewer whether or not you should continue.
- Sit in a professional, attentive manner.
- Ask open-ended questions. You may discover that interviewers enjoy talking about themselves.
- Review your resume and anticipate questions about your duties. Be prepared to answer questions about gaps in employment, changes you have made, and lack of career progression.
- Conduct research and prepare as many good questions as possible. Writing the questions out beforehand helps some people remember them better.
- Ask for the job when you feel that the time is appropriate—at least part of the way into the interview process.
- Ask the employers some type of closing question, if only subtly. For example: "What is the next step?"; "How do I

stack up against the competition?"; "What other information do you need from me?"; or "When do I start?"

- Ask questions that help to distinguish you from other candidates.
- Make sure that the interviewer knows you're willing to leave your teaching career. Be prepared to have that challenged and be able to answer why.
- Be sure to portray yourself as a team player.
- Present yourself as a dedicated, loyal, trustworthy person who is willing to put forth the extra effort to complete assigned tasks.
- Feel free to ask, "Why is this position open?"
- Respond to each question in a timely manner, and avoid "yes" and "no" answers.
- Don't be afraid to respond "no" or "I don't know," rather than beat around the bush or appear as if you know when you really don't.
- Follow instructions carefully and perform to the best of your ability if you are required to take a test.
- Be prepared to present your strengths as well as weakness(es). There is no problem with presenting a weakness, especially if you have identified it and have been working to improve it.
- Upon leaving an interview, be sure to offer a handshake and a polite "Thank you for your time."
- Send a brief thank-you follow-up letter in a timely fashion to each interviewer, if possible, or at least to the main hiring authority. This could be done via e-mail or post office mail. Be sure to carefully check the note for spelling or grammar errors.
- Follow up in a professional manner after each step of the interview.

Don't

- Wear loud or flashy clothing.
- Overdo it with make-up, cologne, or excessive jewelry.

- Assume that a follow-up interview means that you're gaining ground.
- Smoke or have smoke on your breath.
- Have gum, candy, or anything else in your mouth.
- Get off on a tangent and begin to ramble.
- Speak negatively or too critically of any past or current employer.
- Bring up compensation or benefits throughout the interview process. However, when asked the salary question, try to keep the door open for negotiations. If asked a question such as "What salary are you seeking?" feel free to ask the employer, "What range are you offering?" Make sure that the employer feels that your main interest is in the overall opportunity and that compensation is a secondary issue.
- Be afraid to put the interviewer on the spot with a difficult question.

The previous Do's and Don'ts are only guidelines for interviewing. If you become very anxious in an interview situation, just follow these simple rules: Use good common sense and maintain a pleasant, professional attitude, and you will do fine. If you remember nothing else, just be yourself.

Getting Started

You are committed to making a change from your teaching career. You have identified your strengths and selected a career (or careers) that interests you. You have prepared a resume with which you are comfortable. You have rehearsed how to interview effectively. What now?

It's up to you to make something happen. You must be the initiator, the aggressor, and the go-getter. No matter how good the economy is, job opportunities don't grow on trees, no one will knock on your door, nor will a good job be handed to you on a silver platter. You should approach a job search as if it were the toughest task you've ever faced. You should also be prepared to "play a numbers game"—that is, to send out a vast number of resumes, with little positive feedback. You must try to be the eternal optimist. Despite sending out 100 resumes, you have yet to be called for one face-to-face interview. You can't afford to let yourself become frustrated. Yes, it has cost a few bucks, but that 101st resume might result in the interview that leads to a new career. Then, the return on your investment will have been well worth it.

JOB OPPORTUNITIES

The following list provides some ideas about where to find job openings. Remember to constantly be aware of networking opportunities:

- Personal contacts, family, and friends
- Current and former work colleagues
- Public and school libraries
- Career centers and outplacement firms
- Classified ads—national and local newspapers
- Television and radio ads
- Trade magazines
- State employment and unemployment services offices
- Employment agencies and search firms
- Career-consulting firm (be aware that a fee may be charged)
- Community agencies
- The Internet
- Posting your resume at Monster.com and other similar sites
- Professional societies and trade associations—some cities have a group of professionals who exchange ideas at weekly breakfasts or luncheons
- Any government agency

INDEX